*"A highly personal series of reflections explores ways to improve your life.... she deftly describes various tips, she explains that, in all cases, the object is to live the best version of a person's "big" life.... **A warmly written... pep talk for living your "big" life now.***

— *Kirkus Reviews*

"Motivational and hopeful, Nancy Pickard's **Bigger Better Braver** *is a self-help book for those who think that it's too late to change.... The book's progression is logical, beginning with why it's even worth it to work toward such change and then suggesting means of uncovering the unacknowledged beliefs that guide people's decisions... **a self-help companion designed to unearth hope and help it to grow.***"

— *Foreword Reviews*

*"***Bigger, Better, Braver** *is all about stepping out of one's comfort zone to embrace life, and encourages a big leap from set patterns in life to taking on new challenges. It's a top pick for readers who want to make this move, but who don't really know how to do so.... a **highly recommended**, integrative approach that requires that its readers approach life differently.*"

— D. Donovan, Senior Reviewer, ***Midwest Book Review***

"Using her own pivotal experience of climbing Kilimanjaro at 61 years old as the heartbeat of **Bigger Better Braver**, *Nancy Pickard expertly guides us to explore "our own Kilimanjaro." Through client stories and enlivening inner-exercises that magnificently illuminate the path of the most sacred journey we will every take —to self-love and self-worth—**this potent book is a compass I will return to again and again.***

— Nancy Levin, author of ***Setting Boundaries Will Set You Free***

*"Nancy Pickard's extensive training, accompanied by her powerful personal experiences, make this book a must-read for anyone looking to live a **Bigger, Better, Braver** life. Her guidance to dig deeper, discover immense love for yourself, and actionable steps to conquer your fears will take you from 'playing small' to living big and beautifully!"*

— Gina DeVee, author of ***The Audacity to be Queen*** *and founder of* Divine Living

"*They say there's nothing new under the sun… but what if you found what you needed in one place?* **Nancy's step-by-step approach to change** *provides the puzzle pieces that create the inner foundation for successful outer change that is* **Bigger Better and Braver.** *May you* **use this process to create the better story that your life is asking,** *and may that new story equip you to serve the world in the way that only you can.*"

> — Gail Larsen, author of ***Transformational Speaking: If you Want to Change the World, Tell a Better Story***

"*Reading* **Bigger Better Braver** *is like spending time with your greatest cheerleader.* **Truly motivational,** *Nancy Pickard shows us how to override our fears, bust through our excuses, and go for our dreams.* **Filled with relatable stories, tried-and-true teachings, tools, tips, as well as useful exercises and meditations,** *this book supports you in stepping out of your old definition of self and re-thinking your next chapter.*"

> —Kelley Kosow, author of ***The Integrity Advantage***, Speaker and CEO of The Ford Institute

"**If you want more out of life**, *Nancy's book is laying an inspiring path to follow.*

Chock full of examples, practical steps, exercises and cutting edge techniques, she helps you discover your life's calling and coaches you on **how to overcome obstacles and pitfalls on your journey to follow your bliss.**

Her enthusiasm and drive will give you the confidence to take your own leap to make your life happen and manifest what is already inside your heart.

It's what you were born to be. **Highly recommended!**"

> — Teshna Beaulieu D.C., author of ***Fit for Love***

"*Does your life need some basic repairs? Perhaps a complete tear-down and rebuild?* **Nancy provides a toolkit and simple do-able blueprints** *to help you get the job done! Be* **Bigger Braver** *and* **Better** *every day!*"

> — Thomas Crum, author of ***The Magic of Conflict, Journey to Center*** and ***Three Deep Breaths***

"**Bigger Better Braver** *is exactly that! It's a promise kept because Nancy authentically embodies what she presents and backs up her philosophy with* **ideas and ways to activate this in your own life.** *I especially benefitted from examining where I'm on autopilot and checking in on my habits! Perfect timing!*"

> — Becky Robbins, former VP, artist and creator of ***Everything Becky***

"A seasoned life guide, Nancy Pickard helps us see around the blind corners of our personal Kilimanjaro, clear the disempowering brush of our childhoods, and step up to our bigger destiny, all in an **actionable workbook of enabling insights, proven tools, and touching stories.** *Always vulnerable in sharing her own heart challenges, Nancy never stops encouraging us to* **reach for a fuller life and deeper purpose."**

— Steve Engle, CEO

*"***Bigger Better Braver** *captures the fullness of the miracle I experienced working with Nancy Pickard as life coach. She masterfully unraveled the complex puzzle of emotions and disappointments that lurked beneath the surface of my personal façade. In many ways, because of her coaching,* **I feel I owe her my life and the happiness I now enjoy.** *If you want your world to change in positive ways, read this book. It's a true blessing."*

— Kevin Haslebacher, CEO

"Nancy is a fabulous coach that supports you in getting off the hamster wheel to take actionable steps in creating the life you want to live yet can't seem to manifest. **She plants seeds of accountability** *that echo in your ears post-sessions. She points out where you are stuck and encourages you to make lifelong changes.* **She helped me find the courage to leave behind a job that wasn't serving me and create the career of my dreams.** *She rocks and I recommenced her to everyone who wants to live a bigger, Better, Braver life."*

— Crystal Tejera

"Nancy Pickard has written an incredible book. She is the perfect teacher; she has been there. Working with her as a Life coach has been instrumental in my successful navigation through Divorce and Raising Teenagers. She has helped me approach and handle my life's challenges in such a helpful and productive way. **I am more positive, mindful, and peaceful thanks to her.** *Things I admire most about her are her focus... she focuses daily on being better, trying harder, achieving something. I've never met anyone quite as focused as her. She has incredible integrity- always doing what's morally and ethically correct.* **She is brave and fearless...** *she likes to take the path of most resistance in everything she does."*

— Linda Krinsky, Miami, FL

"As you read **Bigger Better Braver** *it's no surprise that Nancy presents a clear path, and 'tools you up,' to take the hike of your life.* **Her direct and relatable style, the stories she shares, and her step by step approach that takes you from "I can't" to "I will" is powerful.** *She has a way of taking the intimidation out of going for your best life, and seeing everything in your path as an invitation to a more expansive you.* **It's a great and effortless read."**

— Linda Yeazel, Master Life Coach

"*Nancy is a wise and thoughtful coach. She guided me through professional and personal challenges with compassion. She demonstrated patience while pushing me to better understand myself and to take action to improve my situation. Her commitment and passion for her work and the process makes her a highly effective coach and I highly recommend her.*"

— Wendy Sherman, Literary Agent, NYC

"*Thanks to Nancy Pickard, **we can all be inspired and supported to live a Bigger, Better, Braver life!** Nancy shares her personal Kilimanjaro while encouraging us to find our own. You will love Nancy's insights and positive energy.*"

— Lauri Boyer, Life Coach

"***Please read this book!*** *Nancy Pickard has written an incredible book. She thoughtfully laid out an actionable plan that anyone can do. **I love this book and am sharing it with everyone I know who wants to live a Bigger, Better, Braver life.***"

— Rev. Laura, Master Life Coach, Trainer, Contributing Author for ***Women Who Rise***

Bigger Better Braver

Conquer Your Fears, Embrace Your Courage,
and Transform Your Life

Bigger Better Braver

Conquer Your Fears, Embrace Your Courage, and Transform Your Life

NANCY PICKARD

TOP READS PUBLISHING, LLC
VISTA, CA USA

First Edition

ISBN: 978-1-970107-12-8 (paperback)
ISBN: 978-1-970107-13-5 (ebook)
ISBN: 978-1-970107-22-7 (audiobook)

Library of Congress Control Number: 2019916476

Bigger Better Braver is published by:
Top Reads Publishing, LLC
1035 E. Vista Way, Suite 205
Vista, CA 92084 USA

For information please direct emails to:
info@topreadspublishing.com

Cover design, book layout and typography: Teri Rider & Associates

Printed in the United States of America

In Memory of my Father,
Irving Gareleck

My father died before this book came to print. I always felt his unconditional pride in me, and I know he watches over me now. I love you Daddy, and a day doesn't go by that you aren't on my mind. I hope we meet again in another life.

Love Always, Nancy

DEDICATIONS

To my parents Claire and Irving Gareleck:
You gave me life and supported my every move.
You taught me to give and receive love and above all,
to trust in myself.

To my beautiful grandchildren, who are our future:
You inspire me to live life to the fullest, and I know you will learn to
trust in yourself and live a courageous and joyous life. Always speak
your truth, be emotionally whole, love yourself, and live life your way.

I look forward to your journeys. You have my heart.

who will you be?

A poem by Nancy Pickard

Your voice
invisible at first
and buried
softer next and heard
over time
bellowing with persistence

quiet the mind
and listen
as your soul speaks
hear it now

the force that stops you
has a name
it's called fear
what's stopping you now

dig deep
uncover
the shadow
that keeps you small

the voice beckons
who will you be
life is meant
to be played
all out

follow your self
be
Bigger
Better
Braver

go now

CONTENTS

INTRODUCTION

Follow your bliss.
If you do follow your bliss,
you put yourself on a kind of track
that has been there all the while waiting for you,
and the life you ought to be living
is the one you are living.

—Joseph Campbell

It was midnight—"summit night"—on Mount Kilimanjaro. Every cell in my body was electrified with anticipation. I had prepared for this moment for six months.

Earlier in the day, we had hiked to 15,000 feet and had dinner at the early hour of 4:00 p.m. Then, we headed to our tents for a final clothing inspection to make sure we were well-protected. I checked and rechecked every detail, savoring a pair of long underwear I'd tucked away for the final climb—an item I purchased because I was told it would hold heat the best in the frigid temperatures.

By 7:00 p.m., coddled in multiple layers of clothing, we all tried to go to sleep. Since I'm hardly accustomed to sleeping at that hour, I barely managed to drift off until we were rustled back to life at 11:00 p.m. It was time for the long-awaited and hard-earned midnight climb to the summit. Everyone in our camp was primed, and the excitement was palpable.

We had spent six grueling days of hiking and contending with the elements to reach our 15,000-feet location. During those six days, everyone in our group—one by one—got sick.

Everyone except me.

I wasn't the eldest in the group at 61. Our team leader was 62, while the rest were in their 30s, 40s, and 50s. I felt proud for making it through without illness. But then, as a retired personal trainer, I knew how to train. I had prepared well and brought immune supplements with me. This planning, along with living part of the year in high altitude, spared me the suffering others endured.

The Kilimanjaro ascent was my 60th birthday present to myself—a formidable challenge that fueled my spiritual quest for self-actualization. I wanted to place myself well outside of my comfort zone in an environment that would push me to my limits and allow me to prove to myself what I was capable of. I made such an epic commitment to training that, in fact, the hiking part (altitude notwithstanding) presented only a modest challenge for me. I was much more challenged by the stress of spending six nights in a tent on a mountain, climbing with the other members of the team, and tending to my own needs and health. But those challenges helped me to trust myself and my abilities. I learned more about my resilience each day.

By day two of our hike up the mountain, I'd learned that I had a much quicker gait than most of our team. So to accommodate my faster pace, I started my climb on summit night an hour after the rest, alongside my guide, to make sure I didn't reach the summit too quickly, as it would have been dangerous to stay up there too long.

Plus, they wanted us to reach it at the same time to take a group photo. Even with starting later, I kept catching the rest of the group and taking twenty minute breaks so that I could stay at my own pace.

To prepare for our summit climb, we each strapped on our head lamps and began making our way to 19,341 feet in the pitch darkness. Two people had become too ill and were sent down from 13,000 feet before our last night. But once the summit climb had begun, there was no turning back. We were all going to the top no matter what, even if the porters had to prop us up.

With our multiple layers of clothing, hats, and face coverings, we looked like an ensemble of mummies braving the fierce winds. The darkness enveloped us, and our head lamps were limited help as we navigated sharp rocks and boulders for six hours.

An hour into the climb, we saw blasts of lightning illuminating the sky in rapid succession. The night before, we had come upon a beautiful grave marker honoring someone who had died on the mountain from a bolt of lightning. I couldn't help but think of that climber as I watched the sky's display. It made the night even more eerie.

As we worked our way toward the top, light began to slowly join the darkness. Before long, we witnessed a blazing, rising sun that wrapped around the mountain like a blanket. It was a breathtaking sight that few people in the world will ever see. The sun edged over the horizon, and I became transfixed. It felt like a spiritual moment for the ages.

It's hard to describe the pride I felt standing on that trail and coming close to the end of my journey as I bowed before the sun. I felt as though I was soaking up the presence of the Universe as it told me I had the drive, knowledge, determination, and courage to make this happen.

When the flags that represent the mountain's peak came into clear view, I was so moved that I started to cry uncontrollably. With each step toward the flags, more tears fell. I was both enormously proud and overwhelmed with relief.

Before I embarked on this challenge, I'd hoped to have a deep spiritual transformation during the climb. I didn't know how or if it might happen. But being on top of that beautiful mountain in Africa at that stage in my life precisely satisfied my spiritual quest. I looked at the flags flapping in the high-altitude winds, and my entire being was filled with an indescribable feeling of spiritual awakening. The mountain pinnacle symbolized the pinnacle of my healing and the reclaiming of the self-love I'd lost at some point in my life.

When climbing Kilimanjaro, you stay no more than a half hour at the peak, where the altitude can make you ill quickly. Many people on our team succumbed to the altitude and the physical exertion. Some made it to the top but struggled to get back down to 15,000 feet without the help of one or two porters to hold them up. One young man even began vomiting blood.

We rested for only an hour at 15,000 feet before packing up and hiking back down to 10,000 feet. Summit Day is a sixteen hour day—an unbelievable grind.

As we approached 10,000 feet where our hike would come to an end for the day, my 61-year-old body began to feel the toll of the cumulative pounding. My body swelled in various places, and my lips became dry and burnt even though they were covered the entire time.

The earlier adrenaline rush left me, and I felt pain throughout my body as if I had been pummeled by a ton of bricks. The pain surprised me, and I was shocked by the appearance of my swollen body in the mirror. It took me days to decompress from the experience, and my adrenal glands were affected for months.

So why would I attempt such a thing? I mean, to a lot of people, climbing Kilimanjaro at age 61 sounds crazy, right? Well, I had decided I no longer wanted to live up to a fraction of my potential in this life. I wanted to eke out every ounce of living I could get and make the most of my time on this earth.

Challenging myself to that degree was a truly transformative experience that was worth the recovery period.

I began the climb as one person. I returned another.

WHAT'S *YOUR* KILIMANJARO?

What about you? Is there something you'd love to do but haven't found the courage? Do you long for a transformative experience? For a bigger, better, braver life—"the three B's"? In other words, what's *your* Kilimanjaro?

Maybe you don't know yet what your own version of climbing a mountain might be. Maybe all you know is that you're tired of living small. Maybe you're sick of feeling timid in your life, letting your fears hold you back from what you could accomplish if you were *only brave enough*. Maybe you look at the lives of others and think they're happier, more accomplished, and living the life you dream of having.

Do you want to feel free and open to experiencing all this world has to offer you? Do you want to give yourself over to the fullest possible experience of living? Do you want to take a leap toward a bigger, better, braver life?

When I talk about living a "bigger, better, braver" life, I'm not suggesting you have to climb a mountain. I'm also not talking about becoming a millionaire or having a mansion in Beverly Hills (although if that's what you want, go for it!)

Your version of a bigger life could be anything! Whatever it is, it will bring you a feeling of elation, accomplishment, fulfillment, and connection with the spirit of who you truly are. It will increase your self-love and introduce you to your soul. These are the real gifts of being brave so that you can live a bigger life—the life I believe you're meant to live. The life I believe your soul is calling you to create.

That's what this book is designed to help you discover—the life that's calling you in a voice that's perhaps getting louder and harder for you to ignore. It's the voice of the big, beautiful, juicy life that's waiting just for you.

Maybe you're thinking, "Sure, Nancy, that's fine and good. You were probably born brave. I don't know that I'll ever have the courage to do something different in my life, no matter how much I want it."

Me? Born brave? That's funny.

MY JOURNEY TO A BIG LIFE

Most of my life, I had no desire to become anything but a wife and mother. I got married and allowed my husband to support me financially. When I had my sons, my husband wanted me to stay at home and raise them, and I was happy to do so. Once they were in middle school, however, I got the itch to work. My husband pushed back, reasoning that he could make more money in one day than I could make in a year. He didn't want my working to change our lives or affect our sons. So I opened a private, personal gym at home. I loved training others and being of service to them. Still, my family remained my priority.

Then, after twenty-six years of marriage, my husband told me he wanted a divorce. It was my own personal earthquake, as if the ground gave way beneath me. I was devastated and utterly lost. Without a man in my life—more specifically, *that* man—I didn't know what to do.

My life was a reflection of my husband's life, and I had no concept of anything different. My mindset was that I needed a man to take care of me; I needed a man to feel whole. The idea that my life could be bigger or could be of my own creation never entered my head. Women who traveled alone impressed me, and I longed to have that kind of courage. But I couldn't muster the drive to do it myself.

After my husband and I split, I dated a lot, moving in and out of relationships, but I was stuck feeling like a victim. In my mind, everyone else was to blame for my problems, and I felt like the Universe had a vendetta against me.

Eventually, I let my gym go and moved to Aspen, Colorado. I met someone new there and became engaged again, finally feeling that my life was back on track.

Then … we broke up. This time, I was forced to wake up and face myself. Surely, the Universe was trying to tell me something. Whatever I received or accomplished in my life was going to be up to me. It was finally crystal clear that I could no longer count on someone else to provide it.

Around this time, someone suggested a book to me by Debbie Ford called *Spiritual Divorce: Divorce as a Catalyst for an Extraordinary Life.*[2] Then, synchronistically, I met a couple of other people who mentioned Debbie to me. As soon as I read the book, I knew I not only wanted to work with a coach from The Ford Institute, but I wanted to become one myself. I had already been doing some work as a wellness coach, but I hadn't thought of it as a career. I'd been stuck in my old mindset, but I was beginning to see other possibilities ahead of me.

Thus began my journey to redefine my life. My victim mindset had been like glue that kept me in an old, worn-out paradigm. Since I didn't know who I was, and I didn't love myself, I felt I needed a man whose reflection of me would help me feel whole. As long as he saw me as worthy, I could see myself as worthy.

When the two men I loved no longer saw me as worthy enough, that reflection shattered like a broken mirror. And no matter who else praised me, their words just bounced right off me and never made a dent in my own lack of self-worth. Believing I was worthy only if they deemed me to be had robbed me of the freedom to create a joyful, inspiring, and extraordinary life. It was only through working on myself and my deeply held beliefs that I realized no one else's opinion of me had any bearing on my value as a human being.

In the years since that awakening, I've obtained five coaching certifications. I worked my way up in The Ford Institute from being a mentor with the organization to Lead Mentor to now Head of Mentor Training. I started writing blogs and doing guest appearances on podcasts, and now I've written a book! I have a career that brings me enormous fulfillment, as well as financial satisfaction. Sometimes, I can't believe how far I've come. It's a wonderful feeling that I so wish for you!

I also travel by myself all the time and love it! And I regularly work on conquering my fears, whether they're physical ones or the result of beliefs standing in my way. I'm a work-in-progress, as are we all, but my life is millions of miles from where I started my adulthood.

In my career as a coach, I've had the pleasure of helping others create their own bigger, better, braver life, too! My clients and I are now dedicated to living as big and brave as we can muster. We will wring as much juiciness out of this life as we possibly can. It's a wonderful way to live, and I encourage you to stick with me on this journey of discovery. Don't sell yourself short. I know without a shadow of a doubt that you're capable of much more than you ever imagined. If I can do it, so can you!

WHAT TO EXPECT FROM THIS PROCESS

The chapters that follow will take you through a tried and true, step-by-step process that my clients have used to discover and design their bigger, better, braver life. Each of them has taken an important leap toward something new and bigger that they wanted for themselves. Through their stories, my personal stories, lessons, interactive exercises, and meditations, you will:

- Uncover a vision of what living bigger means to *you* in your heart and soul. You'll discover how your soul wants to dance.

- Get out of your own way so that you can put your vision for your leap toward a bigger life into action. You'll let go of the habit of operating on autopilot and get unstuck from your old ways of thinking and behaving.

- Strengthen the qualities you need to step into your bigger, better, braver life.

- No longer envy others who have the courage to live big because you will be one of them!

- Cultivate radical courage and become braver than you've been.

- Take your leap toward the change you want in your life.

Here's the plan:

Chapter 1—Why Live Bigger? We'll talk about why living a bigger life is important and explore how to step out of your comfort zone. You'll also find out that you've been more courageous in your life than you thought!

Chapter 2—Get Out of Autopilot. How much of your life do you spend in autopilot? You'll find out in this chapter and learn how to be more present, as well as how to receive messages from your intuition and the Universe to help you achieve your vision and take your leap. (Note that I will use "Universe" throughout the book, but you can substitute God or whatever other word you prefer.)

Chapter 3—Resistance and Excuses to Acceptance and Surrender. We resist what we fear, which keeps us playing small in life, and we make excuses to avoid taking risks. In Chapter 3, you'll release resistance and learn how acceptance and surrender will help you live bigger, better, and braver.

Chapter 4—Uncover Your Vision. What do you really want? How do you distinguish between your soul's vision and your ego's vision? This is just part of what we'll discuss in Chapter 4. You'll create your vision for your bigger, better, braver life and create some action steps to move you in that direction.

Chapter 5—Planning Your Leap. Planning is very important. Taking a leap toward your vision doesn't mean you leap blindly! So in this chapter, you'll create longer-term action steps, while also guarding against getting stuck in the planning phase.

Chapter 6—Understand Faith and Fear. What is the nature of fear, and how can you cultivate more faith and courage? You'll learn how to do just that in this chapter, as well as how to make fear your friend. I'll also introduce the Etching technique.

Chapter 7—Discover Your Unconscious Beliefs. Shadow beliefs are one of the biggest obstacles that stand in the way of your biggest and best life. You'll learn how to discover the beliefs that are holding you back and how to take back the projection of your shadow. I'll also introduce the Tapping (EFT) technique.

Chapter 8—Explore the Unconscious Commitments You've Made. Exploring the commitments you've made unconsciously is one of the most powerful methods for changing your life and taking your leap toward your vision. This is a game-changer that will make all the difference in moving toward your bigger, better, braver life.

Chapter 9—Staying the Course. Do you tend to quit or persevere? As you move toward your vision and create your bigger life, you have to guard against getting discouraged. In this chapter, you'll learn some important strategies to stay the course from maintaining low attachment to the outcome to getting feedback, as well as staying disciplined and responsible to yourself.

Chapter 10—Just Step in and Take Your Leap. In this final chapter, we'll talk about the crucial step of actually taking your leap. Otherwise, you can get stuck in the "honeymoon phase" of planning and moving toward your vision without truly changing your life. Bigger, better, and braver requires action!

That said, I recommend you read this book through to the end before you make a major change. Along the way, you'll be instructed to take some action steps toward your vision, but I advise you to take your final leap after you've completed the chapters. That will set you up for a greater chance of success.

Here's a secret, however: *Everything you need is already inside your heart.* You just need to get quiet and let it be revealed from your inner wisdom. This book will simply help you uncover what is already there.

You deserve the best possible life you can have—let's work together to make sure you have it! In fact, I suggest making this your daily mantra:

BIGGER, BETTER, BRAVER!

1

WHY LIVE BIGGER?

*The saddest summary of a life contains
three descriptions: could have, might have,
and should have.*

—Louis E. Boone

I was brought up in a family of three girls who were taught we could do anything we wanted. At the same time, we were told we should choose a career more in line with conventional expectations for women. Originally, I wanted to be a lawyer, but my mother said, "That isn't a good job for a wife and mother."

Going along with her direction, I went to school to become a teacher, but my childhood programming had worked well. So I transitioned without a hitch to wife and mother. And truthfully, it fulfilled me.

In my marriage, I was a lacrosse and football mom, and I ran fundraisers. I was constantly busy with the kids, our home, and the community. When my sons entered high school, I opened my personal training gym but scheduled my hours around my families' needs. I was happy enough, so I didn't search for possibilities beyond the life I'd created. My childhood reflected my parents' wants and needs, and my marriage reflected my husband's wants and needs. My own desires took such a back seat that I never spent much time evaluating what they were.

Many years after my marriage fell apart and I became a life coach, I had a session with an astrologer. "You haven't self-actualized in any of your past lives. This is the first one for you, and your self-actualization will have to do with spirituality, education, and helping others," she said.

When I told her I had become an integrative spiritual life coach, she added, "You're doing exactly what you're meant to do."

As you know from my story in the Introduction, it took some major kicks in the pants for me to let go of my childhood programming and discover I could have a bigger, better, more fulfilling life. That's true for many of us. The expectations of our families and society often dictate our life choices. We're taught not to strive for "too much" on the off chance we might be disappointed, and we accept these low expectations without challenge. We don't take into account the grave disappointment that comes from a lifetime of never trying to reach beyond those low expectations.

As a result, we go through life unaware there's anything better available for us. We allow fear to direct our actions day-to-day and stifle the inner wisdom that would guide us toward growth and expansion—toward the bigger life that's our birthright. Fear also cuts us off from what we want, shutting down our passion. We don't want to hear that little voice inside that's begging for something more, and the only way to silence it is to go numb.

Clients often say to me, "I'm not passionate about anything." That's a symptom of putting a lid on our emotions. We work so hard to avoid our feelings that we come to believe we have no passion at all, but that isn't true. No wonder so many of us are bored or depressed!

If we dig deep enough, however, we find great passion hiding underneath the habitual suppression of our emotions. That little voice is still very much alive underneath the numbness. So how do we begin to break out of the habitual confines of fear to reconnect with our inner wisdom and passion? How do we hear that voice again?

Keep reading. This book is designed to help you do that and more. These pages will help you reconnect with the truth of who you are and what your soul wants for you. This reconnection process requires inner exploration. Living bigger isn't something we do easily. We've been taught to surrender to fear, not to the wisdom of that voice within. But all fear knows is that it's afraid. It has no other information or knowledge. It only looks at negative possibilities and lives in the darkness. As Jack Canfield and other motivational speakers have put it, "Everything you want is on the other side of fear."

What would happen if you turned your attention toward the light of positive possibilities instead?

When you reconnect with the deepest part of yourself, you discover what you're truly longing for. That inner voice may at first sound small and faint, but the closer and more intently you listen, the crisper and clearer it will become.

Reconnecting with your inner wisdom aligns you with what your heart and soul want for you. From that place of alignment, you'll make wiser choices that will move you toward a larger vision for yourself, and your life will start to fall into place. Does that mean you'll never be challenged or experience an obstacle? Of course not. But you'll find that the challenges and obstacles tend to be shorter term. When you're in alignment with your desire for a bigger life, the Universe will shine brightly to reveal the right path for you and affirm where you need to go.

Exercise: Who You Used to Be

We come into the world believing we can do anything. Then, we conform to what we believe our families or others want, to hopefully be loved and cared for. The following homework exercise will reconnect you with the child you were so that you can begin to recreate that all-important alignment with your heart and soul.

1. Find a photo of yourself as a child at any age, but the younger the better. Frame it, and keep it next to your bed, on your desk, or in another convenient location. Each night, look at the photo. Ask your inner child what they wanted to do or be before you started to mold yourself into what others wanted for you. I'm not talking about a profession like what you wanted to be when you grew up. I'm talking about connecting with who you were and how you saw yourself. You might need to go back to a very young age.

2. Don't worry if you don't have direct memories from when you were very young. Trust your intuition. Use your imagination to begin a dialogue with this young inner child. Close your eyes and drop down to your inner wisdom. Trust that you can access it. See yourself as a child. What do you look like? What are you wearing? What is your mood? Invite your child self to sit down beside you and have a conversation.

3. Ask your child self how they feel about living a big life. What was your dream when you were their age? Put aside any judgments of feeling silly and go with it. Write down what you hear and keep it for reference later.

YOU OWE IT TO YOURSELF ... AND THE UNIVERSE ... TO STOP PLAYING SMALL

How do you know if you're playing small? Answer this simple question: Are you experiencing as much joy as you'd like in your everyday life? If not, you can be sure that your life could be bigger and better. You can be sure that you could be braver. Playing small is a recipe for not just a humdrum life, but an unhappy one.

Stop and think for a moment: If everyone played small, where would society be right now? We'd be without brilliant artists and the many innovations we enjoy in science, technology, thought—everything. It's the people with the courage to live a big life who bring us progress and beauty.

Nevertheless, living bigger doesn't mean you have to make a life-changing contribution to the world to make a difference. Through just your example, you'll begin to transform the world. When you expand your life, the lives of those around you also expand. It's like when you change your dance steps, your dance partner changes theirs as well.

Each of us has innate gifts to express and share with the world. Our value is indisputable. We all matter and have a unique imprint. We are each an irreplaceable piece of the divine puzzle—a one-of-a-kind expression. We owe it to ourselves and the Universe to play full out!

Remember: In the history of time, there has never been and never will be another YOU.

Those of us committed to living big refuse to squander this life we've been given. We treat it like the amazing gift it is.

Living big allows you to make the most of your life and fill your time with amazing experiences. It's transformative. It increases the joy you're capable of feeling in your life many times over. But the greatest gift of living big is how you feel about yourself when you do it.

When we allow fear to keep us living small, we suffer a huge loss. Our missed opportunities cut at our souls. When asked what they regret most in life, the elderly usually say, "the things I didn't do."

My fellow coach, friend, mentor, and five-time author Nancy Levin said this in her book, *Jump . . . and Your Life Will Appear:* "There is so much more to you than you realize. The person your mind thinks you are is only a fraction of your totality. We are not our identities. All the labels you put on yourself, all the concepts and beliefs you have about who you are actually serve to make you smaller than you truly are."[2]

Let me be clear, however: Living bigger isn't just about fulfilling your "full potential." That implies striving for some kind of "success." Living big may involve success if that's where your passion takes you, but it's more about the experience than the end result.

The journey is more important than the destination, and your intention is more important than what you experience or achieve. If you feel drawn to achievement for your own growth rather than for accolades, by all means follow that call. But when achievement is sought because you feel you must earn love, the drive is based in fear.

If living big is about striving for something, it's for expansion and growth.

Living big is truly its own reward.

It is a declaration to the Universe that you are worthy and ready to take advantage of this great gift of life you've been given.

Keep in mind, however, that saying you want to live big and letting go of the fears that have stopped you, perhaps for years, are two different things. That's why, as you continue reading this book, you'll not only work through some of your fears, but you'll also build your courage.

THE COURAGE TO PLAY BIG

There are two different kinds of courage. One is where you take the hand of your fear and take action anyway. You "gut it out." I've used this kind of courage many times, putting on my "big girl pants" when I ski down a double black diamond run on a mountain, take part in a marathon or triathlon, and certainly when I climbed Kilimanjaro. I use it when I travel alone because that always brings up my fears … or when I'm a keynote speaker in front of many. When I push through my fears and do what I want anyway, it proves to me I can do it.

The second kind of courage comes from trust and faith. It comes from knowing that you're part of the divine design. You may not own this belief yet, but developing it is exactly what's needed to feel supported by a strength greater than your own. It's a game-changer!

This second brand of courage comes from knowing that the Universe has your back. It's trusting that everything that has ever happened to you occurred for the evolution of your soul. It means you were meant to take each leap, whether or not they led where you wanted. You still learned something important you could use for your next leap. When you surrender to this, knowing that everything is for your greater good, your courage is based on trust.

It's a courage mindset, which is an act of self-love. When you have that mindset, you recognize who you are and have the passion to step into what you want to do. Passion alone isn't enough. You need the faith that buoys your courage, as well as the discipline to take determined action.

Even taking one step will help you build your courage. In doing so, you declare to the Universe and yourself that you're worthy. The mere act of leaping and landing is transformational and valuable of itself, regardless of what the action brings.

We have to muster the courage to push ourselves out of the nest. Nothing happens until we take that first step toward bigger possibilities. We don't have to know what will happen because we can't know what will happen. In fact, that's a big part of the excitement, isn't it? Wouldn't life be unbearably boring if we always knew what was going to happen next? But that's what fear does. It tells us we should stay safe and embrace only what safety allows. Those efforts are in vain.

Fear often tries to rein us in through comparison. It tells us that other people are more talented and smarter than we are, so what business do we have following our impulses? We have to learn to stop comparing ourselves with others. Author and educator Henry Van Dyke said, "The woods would be very silent if no birds sang there except those that sang best."[3] Stop for a moment and let that in. It's a profound truth.

So rather than think, "I can't" … it's time to think "Why can't I?" Rather than think, "What if something awful happens?" … it's time to think "What if something wonderful happens?"

STEPPING OUTSIDE OF YOUR COMFORT ZONE

One reason we play small is the arbitrary comfort zone we construct based on our childhood upbringing and the avoidance of pain. For example, if you experienced humiliation at a party when you were young, you may find reasons to avoid parties the rest of your life. If you gave a presentation in front of a class when you were a child, and the other kids laughed at you, you might spend the rest of your life avoiding public speaking. The incident may no longer be in your conscious mind, but its memory in your unconscious mind rules your life. This forces you to live within the confines of your comfort zone, missing out on the benefits of living big.

When fearful, we tend to avoid the unknown even more. The voice of our inner fear deems anything outside of our experience as dangerous. Therefore, we feel uncomfortable, and we avoid it.

Sometimes, feeling uncomfortable is a good thing! It means we're trying something new. So the resulting discomfort is natural. In fact, handling fear requires getting comfortable with what is uncomfortable for you. This, in turn, requires having the courage to approach the edges of your comfort zone and take decisive steps beyond it, where an array of personal rewards awaits.

For example, if my client Amanda hadn't had the courage to step out of her comfort zone, she would have missed out on the exciting big life she's created for herself.

Two years after Amanda graduated from college, she was living in Atlanta, working at what she thought was her dream job and enjoying a great social life with a community of friends. "Out of nowhere, I started to feel a nudge to quit my job and move," she says. "I tried to dismiss this thought, but my dismissal came from my fear of the unknown. As the feeling wouldn't go away, I found myself at a crossroads—faced with an uncomfortable change on the horizon."

She reached out to her mother, who sent her the book by Susan Jeffers called *Feel the Fear and Do it Anyway*.[4] "I read it cover to cover and decided to never let fear stop me from living my best life. I would simply find a way to walk through the fear. I gave my two weeks' notice at my job, packed up my belongings, and left," Amanda says.

The move was more exciting than she dreamed it would be! "I quickly got a job working for startup entrepreneur Mark Cuban, and three years later, when AudioNet was sold to Yahoo!, my stock options vested," she says. "As a result, I was able to buy a beautiful townhouse, a brand new car, and completely pay off my student loans from college. Not only that, but one month later, I met the man of my dreams. We've now been very happily married for almost seventeen years. And all because I stepped through fear and outside of my comfort zone." Note that she says she stepped *through* her fear. It was there; she just didn't let it stop her.

Ever since that experience, Amanda has lived by the motto coined by Neale Donald Walsch, the author of *Conversations with God*, "Life begins at the end of your comfort zone."[5]

"Living outside my comfort zone has become a way of life for me, and I can't imagine living any other way. The rewards on the other side are too great to pass up just because of a little fear or uncertainty," she says.

She has continued to live a big life in a myriad of ways. "A few years ago, a friend asked me if I wanted to lead a Bible study at a women's jail, and I found myself saying 'yes' almost immediately. As I walked through the steel doors on that very first day we taught, I felt an uncomfortable nervousness that is hard to describe. Being locked in a large cell with fifty-five female convicts is unnerving and slightly intimidating. This became our routine every other Monday for almost two and a half years, and I have to say it has been one of the most fulfilling, life-changing things I have ever done. To say those women blessed me in a far greater way than I blessed them is simply an understatement."

Amanda has also run 5K and 10K races, half-marathons, and full marathons, followed by triathlons when she "got tired of just running." She had to step through her fear again to sign up for her first triathlon. "I decided to jump in and just start somewhere even though I didn't have all the pieces figured out yet," she says. "I signed up for the Ironman 70.3 Tempe, Arizona race, hired a coach, started swimming laps, and began to research bikes. The date was set, and all I had to do was just show up each day and be excited about the journey."

Since then, Amanda has completed two Ironman 70.3 races and anxiously awaits her next adventure.

What about you? Does Amanda's life excite you or frighten you? If you think of yourself as someone who isn't courageous enough to live big, let's challenge that belief.

Exercise: Courage Recall

I ask many of my clients to make a list of five times in their life they were afraid to do something but did it anyway. Usually, after reading the list, they say something like, "These were the five greatest things I've ever done in my life." Let's discover if that's also true for you.

1. Make your own list of five things you've done in your life that you were afraid to do but did them anyway. Don't limit this list to big experiences of bravery. If you were at all afraid and took action anyway, you displayed courage! You already have everything you need inside you—it's just a matter of gaining access to it. Here are some examples of courageous acts you might include:

    I told my friend I was upset by her comment about my hair.

    I went to the gym even though I felt self-conscious.

    I took a class despite feeling too old to be there.

    I went to a party even though I felt inferior to other people there.

    I left the comfort of my relationship for the unknown.

    I took a new job I feared I couldn't pull off.

    I had dinner alone in a restaurant.

    I signed up for a photography course.

    _____

    _____

    _____

    _____

    _____

2. After you've completed your list, go back and read all its items. Do you see yourself as more courageous simply by remembering these moments when you took action in spite of your fear? How does it make you feel about yourself?

_____

_____

_____

_____

_____

3. For each item on the list, try to recall the courage you felt. See if you can bring on that brave feeling again. Close your eyes, and recall the sights, smells, and sounds of that time.

4. Then, open your eyes and write down what you remember. The next time you feel like you aren't a courageous person, or you need to boost your courage for something you want to do, reread this list and what you remember about those experiences. Bring on that feeling of bravery again to the best of your ability.

_____

_____

_____

_____

_____

POINTS TO REMEMBER

All fear knows is that it's afraid. It has no other information or knowledge. It only looks at negative possibilities and lives in the darkness.

Reconnecting with your inner wisdom aligns you with what your heart and soul want for you.

In the history of time, there has never been and never will be another YOU.

Living big allows you to make the most of your life and fill your time with amazing experiences.

BIGGER, BETTER, BRAVER MANTRA ACTION

Look for some pretty graphics online in beautiful colors with pictures that make you happy.

Type out the letters Bigger, Better, Braver and add to your collage.

Print and post it on your wall where you'll see it every day.

2

GET OUT OF AUTOPILOT

*You are in prison. If you wish to get out of prison,
the first thing you must do is realize that you are in prison.
If you think you are free, you can't escape.*

—G.I. Gurdjieff

Studies show that we are conscious of what we do only about 50% of the time and go through the balance of our lives robotically and on automatic pilot. Think about that for a second: *50% of our lives are lived mindlessly!*

You'll recognize this experience from the habit of driving without thinking. How often do you unconsciously start the car, put your foot on the pedal, and drive your route so zoned out that you arrive at your destination without remembering anything about the trip that got you there? Granted, being able to drive without thinking about each step is a good skill to have. You don't want to have to stop to think about the steps of driving. But it's different when we extend this mindlessness to other parts of our lives like sitting in front of the TV while eating chips, only to realize that all of a sudden, the bag is empty. Or following the same patterns without contemplating how we could expand and grow. When we do this kind of thing, we end up wasting the precious hours we're given.

Moments in autopilot here and there are harmless enough and even beneficial, but staying in that state most of the time means we cut off our connections with others, push away our emotions, and go into long-term denial. That was the case with my friend David, who's a great guy. He also had a terrific job when I met him. But I watched him become sadder and sadder over a period of years.

Finally, one day, when we were bike riding with friends, I rode up next to him and asked, "David, you're so unhappy. How long do you want to stay that way?" I offered to help, and he agreed to coaching.

At first, he felt the problem might be his relationship. He and his wife were polar opposites. He's outgoing; she's an introvert. He likes riding bikes; she likes golfing. It took only a couple of weeks of coaching, however, for him to realize the problem wasn't his relationship or his wife. It was his almost constant state of autopilot—a mindset that prevented him from connecting with what he *truly* wanted and needed to change in his life.

He realized that he hated his job, but he had a lot of fears and beliefs that had kept him stuck there for many years. He was so busy doing the same thing each day that he hadn't stopped to think there could be another way.

Once he stepped out of autopilot and examined what he wanted, he was able to make an important leap in his life, which got him out of that job and changed everything. It's hard to believe, but within a week of leaving his old job, David was able to take advantage of two new career opportunities. He has never been as happy, financially successful, or proud of himself as he has been since he left autopilot behind and took his leap toward a bigger, better, braver life.

And he and his wife are doing great!

For many of us, autopilot is like a hamster wheel. We're running and running and think we're getting somewhere. But we're running in place, doing the same thing repeatedly by rote. A part of us feels we don't have options, so we get up each morning and continue down the same path.

As Kelley Kosow, author and CEO of The Ford Institute, puts it, "Creatures of habit are so busy doing what they have always done that they become oblivious to what they are doing, their motivation, whether their actions serve their highest purpose, and, when it comes to relationships, whether they fuel their flame and are truly healthy."[2]

Why do we do this? The main reason we stay in autopilot is fear—a pervasive and controlling voice in our heads, whether we recognize it as such or not. We might not realize we're afraid. We might think, "Oh, I'm just lazy." But laziness is lethargy or lack of drive that masks the underlying fear. We're terrified to risk stepping into the unknown to try something new.

My client Paul lives in a debilitating state of fear. He feels invisible. Yet, he cowers from spending time with people, reinforcing the very invisibility he wants so much to escape. We spent some time working on his issues in our coaching sessions, but when he decided to stop coaching and tried to continue on his own, he fell back into autopilot and his old habits of avoiding people. That cycle has repeated a few times now, and it's heartbreaking to witness. But he has to be willing to change. He must be willing to recognize when he's giving in to autopilot.

His situation begs this question: Could it be that sometimes our unhappiness has little, if anything, to do with outward circumstances and more to do with our habit of zoning out and not staying present in the moment? I think this is worth considering.

Now, don't get me wrong. I'm not proposing we try to be present each moment of the day. If we did, we'd get nothing done. Nor would we be able to create a vision for the future. Autopilot has value in some circumstances. It allows us to operate on different levels at the same time. It can make us efficient and effective when completing tasks.

If we become more aware of when and how we go into autopilot, we can shut it off when it makes sense and become more present to our experience. The most important thing is to avoid *emotional* autopilot. When we shut down on an emotional level, it's difficult to remain healthy.

We can't possibly connect with what would bring us joy when we're stuck in a robotic way of being. We can't conceive and move toward a vision when we're disconnected from life. Happiness will stay illusive unless we become more aware and mindful of what we're doing and how we feel.

Rebecca Crane, author of *Mindfulness-Based Cognitive Therapy*, says, "Mindfulness encourages us to *intentionally* disengage from automatic pilot and bring our full awareness back to the here and now. By doing this, we open up the full range of possibilities of how we can meet the present moment with absolute intention and awareness." [3]

Everyone has their own brand of autopilot. When I go into that state, I tend to make mistakes because I fail to concentrate on what I'm doing. I overlook important information, and I lose things. I often over-exercise and overdo, trying to be super woman until my body shuts down with an injury, illness, or exhaustion. Someone else's version of autopilot might be the opposite, however—to become a couch potato and do nothing. Let's do an exercise to determine your go-to autopilot behaviors and the habits that get in the way of your best life.

Exercise: Creating New Habits

In this exercise, you'll pay more attention to your habits and decide which ones are standing in your way.

1. During the next seven days, pay attention to your habits. Whenever you catch yourself doing something habitually (you can leave out the common ones like brushing your teeth), make a note of it.

   _____

   _____

   _____

2. At the end of the seven days, look over your list, and divide it into what you consider "good" and "bad" habits. A bad habit prevents you from living your bigger life. For example, during which habits do you go on autopilot?

Good Habits	Bad Habits

3. Write down the day and approximate times of your poor habits or when you went into autopilot each day, as well as what you were doing at the time. These are your go-to autopilot behaviors. Once you know what they are, you can catch yourself and move into mindfulness faster. For example, your go-to behaviors might be:

    a. Binging television shows mindlessly.

    b. Playing games on your phone.

    c. Searching social media.

    d. Tuning out during conversations.

    e. Watching a movie or TV show and realizing you don't know what happened because you weren't paying attention.

    f. Having to reread a book page several times to get the meaning.

Habits	Date / Time

Habits	Date / Time

4. Bear in mind that there isn't anything inherently wrong with any of these actions. Sometimes, you zone out because you're tired or going through something in your life. You may choose to binge-watch a television show to decompress and relax. If you find yourself zoning out more than you'd like, it's good to become aware of the behaviors that lull you into a disconnected state. Awareness is the first step toward being more present during your day!

5. Choose the top two habits you think are hindering you the most. Create a visual reminder that you will see each day to remember to interrupt those habits and step out of autopilot. You could put a paperclip or stone in your pocket that will remind you to check in with yourself each time you touch it. If you don't have pockets, set a frequent alarm on your phone as your reminder.

6. A study published in the *European Journal of Social Psychology* showed that it takes 18-254 days for a new habit to become automatic, with the average being 66 days. It takes an average of 13 weeks to change a habit for life. So be patient with yourself. If you slip up, just try again the next time.[4]

HEARING MESSAGES FROM THE UNIVERSE

One of the gravest dangers of spending too much time in autopilot is not hearing messages the Universe is sending about your vision for your bigger future—about what you can do to make the most of this life you've been given. That was certainly true for David. He was shut down from hearing the messages that he was unhappy in his job.

I believe we're given messages all the time by our inner voice or the Universe that reveal our purpose and attempt to direct us toward our vision. If we're zoned out, we won't notice the messages.

These messages can come in any number of forms. Sometimes, they're loud and bold, while other times, they're quiet and subtle. They can be ordinary, or they can be miraculous like an object that goes missing and then shows up in a place where it would never be. Or a voice you hear in a place where you're alone.

You might, for example, keep seeing or hearing about the same book, which is probably a message to read that book! A friend of mine kept hearing the same song in her head for days on end. No matter how hard she tried, she couldn't replace it with another song. Then, she realized the song lyric was trying to give her a message. A psychic had once told her that her birthright was joy. The song was "Joyful, Joyful," so she finally understood the recurring song in her head was a reminder to not get bogged down by life. To not go into autopilot. It was a reminder to make sure she allowed herself to experience the joy that is her birthright.

Autopilot prevents us from listening to our body, too. The next thing we know, we've run ourselves into the ground and become ill.

These messages can be a big wake-up call for us to make important changes in our lives. Have you ever stayed too long in a relationship or a job, ignoring the nudges you received that you should leave? Would you have been better off if you'd listened and left sooner? Have you ever entered into a relationship or partnership despite the messages you received that it wasn't a good idea? We have all received and chosen to ignore such messages, but the more we stay in autopilot, the more likely these nudges of wisdom will pass by us.

Or we might willfully ignore the messages because of habitual autopilot behavior. My friend says she was feeling down one day because her sister was angry with her. She asked the Universe to lift her energy and help her feel better, but when her request was granted with a cheerful feeling, she almost shifted back into autopilot. She was more comfortable feeling down.

Luckily, she caught herself and remembered she had asked to feel better. She had to laugh at her habit of falling back into her comfort zone of misery. As a result of this awareness, she was able to step out of autopilot and allow the good feelings to take hold.

If we aren't in autopilot, we might also receive messages from the Universe that give us clues about our vision and how to achieve it. When I was working on building my courage and training for the climb, I went to a workshop in which we did fire walking. A man named Wim Hoff was a special guest who talked about taking a group up Kilimanjaro in record time … and while wearing shorts! He also taught a breathing technique, during which he sang the song "Jambo" that the Kilimanjaro guides sing as they climb the mountain. In a room full of thousands, I felt the Universe had sent him specifically for me. It was a very clear message to me that I was to see my Kilimanjaro dream through.

What about you? When in your life have you had an experience that seemed to be a message from the Universe or your intuition?

What signs have you realized later that you missed? What signs might you be missing now? Listening and watching for these messages are among the best ways I know to become clearer about what you want for your big life. You'll have to step into the present and out of autopilot to catch them.

 ## Exercise: Getting Your Messages

This exercise will help you learn to listen to and watch for the messages the Universe sends you.

1. Take a moment to think about the times in your life you didn't listen to the Universe or your intuition. Try to write down at least five examples.

_____

_____

_____

_____

_____

_____

_____

2. For each example, ask yourself what got in your way. What prevented you from noticing? Write down notes for each example. This will help you further determine what habitually stops you from paying attention to the messages you need to hear. Again, awareness is the first step to avoiding excessive time in autopilot.

_____

_____

_____

_____

_____

_____

_____

3. As you learn to step out of autopilot more often and alter the behaviors that lull you into a mindless state, begin to ask the Universe for more messages to help you with your vision. Then, of course, pay close attention to your environment, feelings, dreams, and physical sensations. Watch for seeming coincidences and synchronicities and stay open to what you receive. You might want to keep a notebook by your bed to write down any dreams you remember upon awakening. If you don't tend to remember your dreams, keeping the notebook by your bed for a period of time will help you start to remember them. If you'd rather not write them down, record the dreams you recall on your phone.

4. When you notice a sign from the Universe, take a moment to express your gratitude. I actually look up and say, "Thank you, Universe!" The more present and grateful you are for these gifts, the more they will come your way. As you get better at noticing the signs and gifts from the Universe, you may notice they come faster and more easily. Once, I arrived at a gym for a yoga class to discover I'd forgotten to bring a

hair tie with me. When I walked into the locker room, it was empty except for a single hair tie. I looked up and said, "Boy, you work fast. Thank you, Universe!"

AVOIDING ZOMBIE LAND

For Jason, taking care of himself and scheduling in "me" time before his kids wake up each morning helps him avoid zoning out during his day. That time gives him a rejuvenating boost.

"Your dream may just be, 'I don't want to be in pain anymore,'" he says. "It might be as simple as that. You've got to have dreams. Then, I think the other part of it is doing practices that help slow you down and put you in a position of being able to watch your mind, clear your mind, and stabilize your mind. Jason quotes Ram Das when he says: "The mind is a great master but a lousy servant. You want to be the master of your mind, not the servant."

Mastering your mind deserves its own book, but it's one of the key ways to pull yourself out of autopilot or what I call "zombie land." You will no doubt find your own ways to do this, but here are eight ways I've found work well to stay out of zombie land, better receive those important messages from the Universe, and live your life more fully:

1. Each morning before jumping out of bed and hitting the ground running, take a moment to check in with yourself and ask: *What is one thing I can do today to make my day better?* Then, commit to doing that one thing. This simple action gives you the opportunity to go beyond mundane routines and mindless habits, bringing deeper self-awareness that widens the aperture of your day from its beginning.

2. Before you go to sleep, write down three things for which you are grateful from the day. Use colorful construction paper for

these gems rather than plain paper, and place them in a clear jar. Then, write a fourth thing you wish you had done during the day, and commit to seeing it through tomorrow. Your colorful jar will remind you of your gratitude. Even if you've had a dismal day, remember to express gratitude for the roof over your head, the food you eat, and your warm bed.

Gratitude is the key to positive energy and avoiding zombie land. When you go to sleep from a place of gratitude, you will sleep better and wake up happier.

Studies have shown that even one grateful thought increases our happiness and reduces depressive symptoms. These effects don't last, however, so to maintain the benefits, we have to feel gratitude regularly.

3. In Debbie Ford's book, *The Right Questions*, she says to make the right choices, you first have to ask yourself the right questions. One of those questions is: "Will this choice propel me toward an inspiring future or keep me stuck in the past?"[5] Asking yourself this will help you avoid making automatic choices based on habit or fear. Bear in mind, too, that no choice is small. Each choice you make matters. Sometimes, seemingly small choices create big outcomes, so making conscious choices will bring you closer to your vision.

4. Practice mindfulness five minutes a day. Simply sit in stillness and stop doing or planning anything. This is *not* autopilot! This is mindful sitting in which you stay present in the moment. You may find it difficult at first, as your habit might be to zone out. Keep reminding yourself to come back to the present. It sometimes helps to notice your body's sensations while you sit still. Even these five minutes daily will make a

difference in your ability to stay out of zombie land. Research has shown that the brains of people who meditate regularly are less prone to wandering, and as they rest, they're more likely to stay present.

5. Practice mindful listening while at a work meeting or during a conversation. Listen intently and notice what you're feeling both emotionally and physically. Make a conscious effort to hear not just the words, but the message that's communicated.

6. To avoid going into autopilot in your relationships, tell a loved one something positive about them or your relationship each day.

7. Make it a point to make eye contact with your loved ones, as well as strangers. Making eye contact affects how you feel about people and pulls you into the present moment and out of zombie land. Try it at the grocery store or while waiting in line anywhere.

8. Put a sticky note on your bathroom mirror that says, "I choose me!" Each morning, using that mirror, look yourself in the eyes and repeat "I choose me" three times. Say it aloud, if possible. If not, you can say it silently to yourself as you brush your hair or your teeth. Affirmations like those, repeated regularly, can have a profound emotional effect on you. If you make this commitment to choose yourself and make choices that align with your soul's vision, you'll feel more energized and much less likely to fall into the zombie zone.

MINDFUL EATING

For Kara Richardson Whitely, author of *Gorge: My Journey Up Kilimanjaro at 300 Pounds,*[6] binging was a common behavior when she went into autopilot. She's far from alone in this practice. It's one of the ways many people cope with emotional pain, but it ultimately causes more emotional pain, as well as physical issues. This is one of the reasons I also recommend practicing mindful eating during one meal a day. Not only will it help you digest food better, it will also teach you how to be more present. Here are some ways to eat mindfully:

1. Chew 20 times before swallowing.

2. Eat silently.

3. Feed yourself with your non-dominant hand.

4. Eat with chopsticks for a day.

5. Put your fork down between each bite.

Getting rid of restrictive habits and avoiding the stranglehold of autopilot means finding the life path that is yours alone. To get there, you need self-awareness, attention to the Universe, a commitment to change, and techniques that are suited for you. It can happen! Give yourself permission to be the warrior you can be because the rewards are there for the taking.

POINTS TO REMEMBER

We can't possibly connect with what would bring us joy when we're stuck in a robotic way of being. Happiness will stay elusive unless we become more aware and mindful of what we're doing and how we feel.

When you notice a sign from the Universe, take a moment to express your gratitude. I actually look up and say, "Thank you, Universe!" The more present and grateful you are for these gifts, the more they will come your way.

Each morning before jumping out of bed and hitting the ground running, take a moment to check in with yourself and ask: *What is one thing I can do today to make my day better?*

Gratitude is the key to positive energy and avoiding zombie land. When you go to sleep from a place of gratitude, you will sleep better and wake up happier.

BIGGER, BETTER, BRAVER MANTRA ACTION

Wim Hoff teaches a breathing technique in which you take 30 quick breaths through your nose and exhale through your mouth. Then, you take a deep breath and exhale, holding the exhale until you have to breathe in again, holding the inhale for 10 seconds.

My sons and I do this breathing method and take ice plunges.

The whole time, I use the Bigger, Better, Braver mantra to keep my breathing calm.

It is invigorating! So at the end of your shower tomorrow, spend the last 15 seconds under cold water.

Use the mantra to calm your breath as you awaken your body, mind, and soul to the new bigger, better, braver you.

3

RESISTANCE AND EXCUSES TO ACCEPTANCE AND SURRENDER

❧

Surrender is deeply misunderstood as an act of weakness.
Surrender is the bravest and most lucid thing a human ever
does, and that's why it's so precious to the Divine.

—Andrew Harvey

When I moved to Aspen, I was like a kid in a candy store because
of all the opportunities for different kinds of exercise. I'd go hiking
with my dog, biking, skiing, and maybe even take a yoga class all in a
single day. I didn't have to work at the time, so I spent my entire days
doing some form of exercise and loved every minute of it.

Paul Chek, a highly regarded trainer and the author of *How to Eat, Move and Be Healthy*, once told me I was working out more than professional athletes. "You look amazing, but you're burning yourself out from the inside out," he said. I just shrugged it off. I was happy and thought he was worrying over nothing.

Then … I got melanoma skin cancer on my leg because I had over-taxed my immune system. I had to have extensive surgery. I couldn't walk for two weeks, let alone hike or work out.

The day after my surgery, while recuperating at my son's house, he sent his meditation coach to work with me. "Don't you find it amazing that the only way the Universe could stop you in your tracks was to give you melanoma?" she said.

"Are you freaking kidding me?" I thought. I couldn't believe she thought my melanoma had anything to do with how much I'd been exercising or that the Universe was in any way involved!

But I have come to understand that she was right. It just took me a while to come to terms with reality. Since then, I've learned that if we don't listen to our body, it will make itself heard in another way.

I wasn't listening. I was too busy enjoying my endorphin high.

It was a classic example of resistance to my highest good, even though I had come up with all sorts of excuses why my excessive exercising was the right thing for me. It took some work, but I was able to stop believing my excuses and let go of resistance. I started to temper my exercise regimen, watching myself to make sure I didn't become excessive again.

I remained careful about over-exercising for years. Then, the time came for me to train for Mount Kilimanjaro. It was too easy to stop listening to my body again and fall back into my old habits. As someone who's addicted to the endorphin high, I was back in my happy place with the excuse I had to train that hard to make sure I reached the top of that mountain.

By the time the climb was over, I had used up all the minerals that support my adrenal glands. Ever since then, I've been fighting to recover from adrenal fatigue.

Don't get me wrong, though: I don't regret taking that leap to climb Kilimanjaro—not at all! I learned that to accomplish it, I didn't have to train as hard as I thought. We all make mistakes along the way and learn important lessons when we go for a bigger life. The leap is still worth it.

And it goes to show that even when we learn a lesson the hard way, our habitual resistance can come up again, forcing us to relearn the lesson.

We are all prone to resistance. It's a defense mechanism we use at various times in our lives—no matter how committed we may be to personal growth and change. This resistance not only prevents us from discovering what would bring us more joy in life, but it gets in the way of our taking action on that discovery.

Ironically, the more we work on transforming ourselves, the more likely we are to resist the changes we want to make. Most parts of us want to change, but other parts of us remain afraid. Those parts feel they have to spare us the potential pain of taking a risk. So resistance almost always results in an internal conflict between the parts of us that are locked in fear and the parts of us that are courageous.

My friend Olivia loves to travel and has been all over the world, often by herself. "A part of me is always resistant to traveling, no matter how many trips I've taken and enjoyed," Olivia says. "This part of me is afraid and lazy all the time. She would be happiest if I never did anything but sit in my easy chair 24 hours a day where, she believes, I would never be in any danger. Her influence is strong, but I know better than to listen to her. Sometimes, I have to placate her fear and tell her it will be okay if I go to Japan or Madagascar by myself. I always take the trip anyway because I know how much travel has enriched my life."

The problem is that these parts of us that believe resistance protects us from pain are wrong. Instead, resistance only prolongs and sometimes even intensifies our pain. Carl Jung, the founder of analytical psychiatry, said, "What we resist persists."[2] The more we resist something, the more it will become a problem in our lives.

Anytime we go into denial or refuse to accept "what is," we're in resistance. It's like swimming upstream against the current. We believe it's easier, but it's much harder. Like what happened to me both times I went into denial about over-exercising, you have probably already had at least one experience in your life in which you denied the truth for a while, only to have that truth bite you in the end.

Here's another example from my own life. After my divorce, I stayed in a new romantic relationship even though I knew it wasn't right for me long-term. I was afraid to be alone and afraid I might not be able to find someone better for me, so I had all sorts of excuses why I needed to stay. I resisted what I knew deep inside was the right choice. Staying with him felt safe in the moment, but I wasn't in integrity with my biggest vision for myself.

How do you know if you're in resistance? If you feel dissatisfied, exhausted, afraid, or stuck, you are probably resisting the truth. If you find yourself complaining, gossiping, overeating, over-exercising, over-planning, overanalyzing, or overworking, you are no doubt in resistance. Remember autopilot? It's a prime example of resistant behavior.

Debbie Ford said, "Resistance is like a beach ball. When you push it under water, it pops back up to the surface even stronger."[3] Not only does it get stronger, but it often pushes back up unexpectedly at the most inappropriate times, such as when you lose your temper. Resistance not only sets you up for more pain in the long run, but it also deprives you of all the choices otherwise available to you. As long as you're in resistance, you're stuck, unable to take the leap you need to create a more fulfilling life for yourself. If it goes unchecked, resistance can cause you to squander your entire life. You deserve so much more than that!

Exercise: Release Resistance

In her book *Mantras in Motion: Manifesting What You Want Through Mindful Movement,* Erin Stutland combines movement with mantras to help you create change in your life by using both your body and your mind.[4] I highly recommend her book, which is filled with mantras and exercises you can do to create what you want. For our purposes, I have put together my own short set of simple movements and a mantra to help you make a commitment to yourself to release your resistance to what is.

1. Hold your arms straight out to your sides, and shake your hands freely as you say aloud, "I let go of my resistance."

2. With your arms still extended out to your sides, make big circles as you say aloud, "I allow my dreams to grow."

3. Bring your hands together in the prayer position in front of your heart and then up to your third eye (your forehead between your eyebrows), and back down to your heart as you say aloud, "My confidence flows within me."

4. Make a fist with each of your hands and punch the air with one hand followed by the other, as you say aloud, "I'm stronger than I know!"

5. Repeat steps 1-4 two more times for a total of three.

6. Go through this cycle once a day for at least two weeks or until you feel you are beginning to let go of your habit of resistance.

EXCUSES–THE LIES WE TELL OURSELVES

Our excuses are the justifications and rationalizations that keep us in resistance and placate the parts of us that are afraid. They're sneaky because they sound reasonable, as they trick us into sidestepping responsibility for what happens to us. They sabotage us so that we don't make the necessary leap to change our life. They derail us with temptations of comfort.

But excuses are nothing more than lies we tell ourselves.

Resignation, for example, is a common excuse. We become resigned to what we believe are a limited number of choices, or perhaps no choices at all. Even if the facts say that our choices are few, there are almost always more possibilities available to us than we allow ourselves to believe or accept.

When we use excuses to stop us from living our big life, we fight for our limitations. We tell ourselves we "can't" or "shouldn't" try something. We tell ourselves we "don't know how" or we are "too old" or we "don't have enough money." We fight to stay a victim, to stay helpless and disheartened because it feels safe. We deny the power we have to change. My client Paul (from Chapter 2) was upset about being invisible, but he was so afraid of change that his resistance kept him invisible. In fact, he fought hard for that invisibility, which gave him a sense of safety that also left him lonely and miserable.

Here's a reality check: If there's something we truly want to do, "can't," "shouldn't," and "don't know how" are just words to mask "won't." My client Steve has a mantra that's a great motivator: "If I can't, I must." In other words, if his resistance tells him that he can't, it's an indicator to him that it's something he *must* do.

For anything we want to do, there will always be obstacles and reasons we can use to prevent us from trying. We will never run out of reasons *not* to do something that feels scary. One of the primary aims of this book is to provide you with several methods for overcoming your fears so that you can take the leap into your biggest imaginable life.

Of course, I'm not suggesting you trample all over the parts of you that are afraid in order to let go of your excuses and conquer your resistance. It's important to feel compassion toward the scared parts of you.

As you move through the chapters of this book, you'll begin to dismantle some of the fears that are holding you back so that you can move forward in spite of them. Like my friend Olivia, you may have to placate parts of you that are afraid and take your leap even with the fear and resistance still in place. Our fears and resistance may ease and become less pronounced, but they never go away entirely. Even after years of traveling, Olivia's resistance is still present. She has simply learned that this resistance isn't in her best interest, so she reminds the fearful parts of her that all will be okay, as she steps on the plane and goes.

Making excuses and avoiding reality are choices we make, so like Olivia, we can make a different choice. We can go along with our resistance, or we can take action despite it.

 Exercise: What Are Your Excuses?

There are no doubt things you've wanted to do but didn't. Let's discover the excuses that prevented you from doing them.

1. Think back on the last five years of your life. Write down five things you wanted to do, but something stopped you.

    _____

    _____

    _____

_____

_____

_____

_____

_____

_____

2. For each of the things you wrote down, make a list of the reasons you told yourself you couldn't do them.

_____

_____

_____

_____

_____

_____

_____

_____

3. Reread each reason. Ask yourself: Is this a fact or an excuse? Be brutally honest here! For example, you might say you wanted to take a trip to Paris, but you didn't have the money. While it may be factual that you didn't have the money, was there a way you could have saved up for the trip if you'd only tried? If you had put a little bit of money aside each month during that

five-year period, could you have gone to Paris? Reflect on your excuses so that you can catch yourself more frequently in the future and allow for more possibility in your life.

4. Please be sure to keep these lists, as I'll ask you to refer to them later!

SURRENDER AND ACCEPTANCE

Tighten both of your hands into fists and hold them tight for at least five seconds. Now, release it, and let your hands relax. Now, tighten every muscle of your whole body. Squint your eyes, lift your shoulders, make a fist with your hands, and curl your toes under. Hold it for five seconds and release. You have just experienced the difference between resistance and surrender. Resistance is a state of tension, while surrender is a state of freedom.

Resistance is like holding your breath, always braced for what might go wrong. You're terrified you're going to have to face the truth. It's the same kind of strain and anxiety you feel when you've lied to someone and you're afraid they'll find out the truth.

When you're in resistance, there's a part of you that knows deep down that your excuses are lies, so there's the constant fear of being forced to face what you don't want to see. A part of you knows you aren't living up to your potential, which causes shame and self-loathing.

I was resistant to doing Facebook Live videos and creating a presence on social media, for example. I had lots of excuses for why I wasn't doing these, but as I watched other coaches promoting themselves and progressing in ways I wasn't, my resistance made me feel bad about myself. Now, I'm doing Facebook challenges and growing my social media platforms in multiple ways. And whatever the ultimate results, I feel great about it. I know I'm taking care of business and doing what I need to do to get myself "out there." I've conquered my resistance and faced the truth about my fears and excuses.

What really happens when you face the truth? There may be momentary pain, but once you've faced it, you no longer have to hold the tension that lying requires. Then, you can move into acceptance, which leads you to the freedom of surrender.

Acceptance means seeing the facts exactly as they are without wishing anything was different. It isn't the same as complacency. You can still change your circumstances, but with acceptance, you'll start your move toward change from a place of absolute truth about what is.

The freedom of surrender can only happen from a place of acceptance because it's only when we accept what is that the tension of resistance can relax.

Surrendering to what is gives us hope and energy that we don't have at our disposal when we're in resistance. It's an active choice. When we surrender to what is, we acknowledge our trust in the Universe and that things will unfold as they are meant to unfold.

Acceptance and surrender allow us to stop being the general manager of our lives. We can trust that the Universe has our back and stop trying to control everything from a place of fear. In Debbie Ford's book, *Courage*, she says, "When you awaken to this true essence that exists inside of you, there is nothing to fear. You suddenly have access to a divine self that is infused with power, confidence, and courage."[5]

This is difficult to do, of course, because our ego, which is fed by our limiting beliefs and fears, wants to be right. It views life through the perspective of the pain and hurt of the wounded child within. It fights for our limitations because that's what helps us feel safe. The ego thinks it's saving us, but it's actually keeping us stuck, sabotaging our growth. So instead of thinking that life happens *to* us, we need to believe that life happens *for* us.

According to the Code of Divine Guidance in Debbie Ford's book, *Courage*, all of us have the Divine within us, and it's constantly guiding us and encouraging us to grow. The more we learn to receive its messages and trust that we're cared for, the more we can surrender to the reality of what is.[6]

In the next section, I'll discuss one of the key ways to move into acceptance and surrender.

THE OBSERVER

When people ask me the biggest transformation I've experienced as a life coach, I say it's learning how to be an observer of my life rather than always the "reactor" to my life. Our default is to react in fear to the events we experience, and we have all sorts of fearful thoughts that often become lifelong beliefs. For example, let's say your father told you that you'd never amount to anything, so every time you try to accomplish something, you come up against your fears and resistance. The voice of your father replays in your mind, telling you that you'll never amount to anything. Your excuses become, "There's no point in trying" or "I'm not smart enough for that."

As you believe your inner voice, you have an emotional reaction to these thoughts. You then believe your excuses, and any action you wanted to take is stopped dead in its tracks.

If you learn to become an *observer* of your life instead of a reactor, however, you will begin to *watch yourself* having these thoughts. You will hear yourself repeating, "You'll never amount to anything" and "There's no point in trying." From that observer place, you can be more objective and question the truth of these thoughts, thereby avoiding the emotional reaction to them. You can say to yourself, "These are excuses and beliefs that aren't real. Dad said that because of his own pain. He couldn't possibly predict what I would be capable of doing as an adult."

This observer part of you will allow you to reinterpret the thoughts, fears, and excuses that have kept you from moving forward in your life. You will begin to notice that you have ascribed meaning to these thoughts that have no basis in objective reality.

This is an important truth: *It isn't what we go through that defines us. What defines us is what we make it mean, coupled with the actions we take.* We have the choice to make our thoughts mean something other than how we may have always interpreted them. Remember that your interpretations of these thoughts probably originated when you were a child with limited understanding of the world or what was possible. You were vulnerable and unable to see with the clarity of an adult. The observer allows you to begin to unravel your thoughts, fears, and excuses from an adult perspective.

Jack Canfield says in his book, *The Success Principles,* that the event + our reaction = the outcome (E+R=O).[7] The event may be out of our control, but our reaction is within our control, and that will make all the difference in the outcome. Many times, we blame ourselves or make ourselves wrong when a painful event occurs. This adds more drama and trauma to the outcome. If, rather than going into autopilot and having a knee-jerk reaction, we step back as the observer and evaluate the event rationally, we can avoid adding more pain to the experience. We can choose not to believe the old, habitual self-talk that makes events mean negative things about us. As Jason said, we can use the observer part of us to make the mind our servant rather than our master.

In his book *The Untethered Soul* (another book I highly recommend), Michael A. Singer said, "There is nothing more important to true growth than realizing that you are not the voice of the mind—you are the one who hears it."[8] This is the power of the observer.

The observer looks at every bump, twist, and turn in life as an opportunity for growth. The observer asks, "What's the lesson here? What's the gift in this experience, even if it's been terribly painful? How can I grow from this experience?"

CHANGING NEURAL PATHWAYS

Studies by neuroscientists show that we can create new neural pathways in the brain by repeating positive thoughts. So affirmations really do work if we repeat them enough, and in the process, we can actually change our brains!

In the last chapter, we talked about habits and autopilot. Our thoughts are so habitual that we tend to think the same ones over and over. So it's up to us to change those habits by thinking new thoughts that serve us better and lead us toward our bigger life. The first step is to become the observer rather than the reactor in order to recognize the thoughts we need to change.

 Meditation: Connecting to the Observer

For this meditation, read through all the steps, and use your memory to walk yourself through them with your eyes closed. Find a quiet, comfortable place to sit by yourself for 15-20 minutes, and turn off all phones.

1. Close your eyes, and settle into your seat. Take a few slow, deep breaths, and connect with your inner wisdom. Place your hand over your heart, and feel it beating. Breathe deeply, and with each inhale, fill your chest and abdomen with air. With each exhale, let your body relax even more.

2. Use your breath to drop down deeper, sending the breath to your heart.

3. Think of an instance in your life in which you experienced conflict. You might have had a disagreement with your boss or an argument with your partner, family member, or friend. Recall what happened during the conflict. Did you react from your gut, or did you take time to let your emotions settle? Can you now look at the event from the observer perspective, without any judgment toward yourself or others, and note the two different possible reactions? What would be the knee-jerk reaction, and what would be the more rational reaction from the observer place? For example, maybe you jumped to the conclusion that your friend doesn't care or doesn't treat you the way you treat her because she wasn't available to help you when you needed her. From the observer place, you might step back and see that perhaps her inability to help in that circumstance had nothing to do with her feelings about you.

4. Take another deep breath, and on the exhale, let go of any judgments that may have come to the surface. Drop down deeper and ask yourself: What is the lesson here? What is the gift?

5. Now, choose another conflict or difficult event you experienced, and go through the same process. How did you react, and could you have reacted in a more loving way as the observer?

6. How can you support yourself in connecting with the observer part of you? Is there a practice you could put into place, such as waiting 24 hours before responding in a heated situation? Perhaps you could ask the other person to give you time before discussing the matter. You could take a deep breath

and ask the observer to be present with you. It might help to disconnect from your emotions temporarily in that moment and become as neutral as possible. Practice connecting with the observer whenever you become upset or put yourself down. Ask yourself if your reaction is true. Ask yourself why the other person may have reacted as they did and whether it had anything to do with you personally. Find your own ways of connecting to this observer part of you.

7. When you're ready, shake your shoulders, roll your head, begin to come back to full waking consciousness, and open your eyes.

POINTS TO REMEMBER

Resistance not only sets us up for more pain in the long run; it also deprives us of all the choices otherwise available to us. When we use excuses to stop us from living our big life, we fight for our limitations.

Acceptance means seeing the facts exactly as they are without wishing anything was different.

Surrendering to what is gives us hope and energy that we don't have at our disposal when we're in resistance.

It isn't what we go through that defines us. What defines us is what we make it mean, coupled with the actions we take.

BIGGER, BETTER, BRAVER MANTRA ACTION

*On your phone or computer, create a
reminder to bring the Bigger, Better, Braver Mantra
to your attention several times a day.*

*There are all sorts of apps to make this happen for you,
and it will keep you on track toward your vision and
your leap.*

4

UNCOVER YOUR VISION

The major reason for setting a goal is for what it makes of you to accomplish it.

What it makes of you will always be the far greater value than what you get.

—Jim Rohn

When Benjamin graduated from college, he lacked all sense of a career path. He stumbled upon an internship that led to a job on Wall Street, but there was nothing purposeful about it. "I woke up one day and felt like the whole thing had just kind of happened," he says.

He looked at the guy sitting next to him, stuck in the job for ten years, and he saw what misery looked like. "The whole environment was so miserable," Benjamin recalls.

He was lost as to what to do, but he continued to receive raises and bonuses at work. "I was wearing custom suits, and I seemed to have a somewhat prestigious position compared to most of my fellow college graduates. There were all these reasons why it seemed like such a great thing, but it also felt useless to be there."

Then, he started seeing a personal trainer and learning about organic foods. To eat healthier, he began to make his own food. Bringing his lunch to work even got him the nickname, "The Weirdo."

Before long, he was practicing mindfulness meditation, blogging about healthy cooking, and coming to terms with the toxicity of his work environment.

He thought about quitting his job and going to culinary school. But his father told him if he left the job for two years to study the culinary arts, only to find he didn't like it, he would have a difficult time returning to Wall Street. So he gave his decision a bit more time.

It didn't take long for him to lose 100% of his interest in his job. All he wanted to do was look up recipes.

"Flash forward a year after," he says. "I was writing the blog, I'd been meditating for a year and a half, and I started to realize it wasn't food and cooking so much that I was attracted to, but farming and sustainable agriculture. Even just nature in general. The reason I liked the food and the cooking was because it gave me a closer connection to nature, to food production, and the source."

Then, Benjamin's father approached him with an idea. He wanted to buy land in Idaho to develop a property with an organic farm, solar panels, and a water supply so that he could be free from the grid whenever he wanted and have a haven in the event of a national disaster. Benjamin had already done enough research on similar properties and how they operate to know how to make it work. "I came up with a concept right on the spot that we would commercialize his vision into a small destination resort that was based on the farm and had guest houses," Benjamin says. "I was thinking 365 days a year, we'd have this amazing business connected to the land that would allow us to have a Wall Street salary but a country lifestyle, which was starting to feel like my goal."

It didn't make any sense for someone from Wall Street with no farming experience to become a farmer, but when Benjamin made the decision to do it, he says, "I felt alive. I just felt like I was living. I felt like I went from sitting in the back seat of a rollercoaster to sprinting in front of a rollercoaster."

Each teacher he needed for his vision to come alive started to come into his life. That often happens when we're in alignment with the vision of our future—with what our soul wants for us. "If I kept going forward and leaning into the vision, everything I needed was right there," Benjamin says. And while it hasn't been easy or without some obstacles along the way, his dream is a dream no longer. It has become the life he lives. The farm, rooted in sustainable agriculture, is flourishing, and the companion luxury resort, geared to provide a transformative hospitality experience, is in progress.

For many of us, like Benjamin and David (from Chapter 2), it simply starts with dissatisfaction. We aren't happy with our life as it stands, or at the very least, it doesn't excite us. Sometimes, the dissatisfaction begins as a low rumbling deep within. We might barely notice it at first, but over time, the rumbling gets louder. Before we know it, it shakes us to the core.

Perhaps the best way to describe this feeling is *restlessness*. At first, we don't know what we want to do that's different. We just know that what we *are* doing isn't working for us anymore.

This is what happens for many of us when our soul taps us on the shoulder and says, "It's time to live bigger. You can't pretend anymore." That's when we need to find a new *vision* for our life like Benjamin did.

Now that you've begun to notice your resistance, excuses, and tendency to go into autopilot, it's time to think about *your* vision for *your* bigger, better, braver life—the future you will create.

THE SOUL'S VISION VS. THE EGO'S VISION

You can't create that vision from the old thinking or the old paradigms. That would only create more of the same dissatisfaction. As Einstein once said, "We cannot solve our problems from the same level of thinking that created them."

That is why so many people turn to vision boards. Some of you have probably already created vision boards, and you may even feel disdainful about them. You might be thinking, "Yes, Nancy, I made one of those, and it didn't work for me." But so often, we create these visions from the mind or the ego, so they become about achievements we "think" we "should" accomplish. Therefore, I recommend digging deeper with a meditation before making your vision board. Then, you'll be more likely to create your vision from your heart and soul. Your soul knows what will not only make you happier, but what will provide the most growth and transformation for you. I call my version of this process the "Soul's Vision Board."

There are some important distinctions between an ego's vision and the soul's vision. For the ego, reaching the goal is paramount. If you don't, you fail. It's black and white with no shades of gray.

For the soul, your *intention*—the vision itself—is paramount. Making it through the climb to the top of Kilimanjaro was very important to me. It was, of course, my vision—something I very much wanted to accomplish for myself. But setting that vision and taking the steps to get there were also transformational for me. I like to say *the juice is in the journey*, but we can't downplay the importance of reaching your own personal summit, whatever that may be. It's just that the soul's vision encompasses all the shades of gray, and failure isn't even in the vocabulary, whether you reach your personal summit or not. There's so much to gain from the journey.

My client Tania wrote a book for which she received significant recognition. That, of course, has been wonderful, but the journey has been the juice for her. "The process of healing and expressing myself were enough. The rest was just a big cherry on a sundae," she says.

The process will only be transformative, however, if you truly go for it and make a commitment to what you have envisioned. Your vision is a gravitational pull—an expansive, big-picture target that you feel a strong impulse toward. Like Benjamin, you may not know why, but the pull is undeniable.

Here's a radical thought: *Your vision doesn't necessarily have to feel real or attainable.* Yes, I really mean that! I could have had the vision to be an actor in movies and set my sights on getting there. Whether I reached the goal or not, the journey in that direction would be a learning experience, stretching me beyond my comfort zone. That is a better place than sitting at home, telling myself I could never become a movie star. (And who's to say it couldn't happen? Stranger things have.)

The bottom line is this: Wherever your soul is pulling you, it's your yellow brick road. Follow it, and see where it leads. Along the way, the vision may change. It could be that seven steps toward one vision, you realize you have a new vision. But you never would have conceived the new vision unless you'd completed those initial seven steps.

What if you feel you have no vision? You know *something* needs to change, but what? Where does your soul want you to go? The next exercise will guide you in a meditation to connect with your vision. If Benjamin had done this exercise, for example, he might have seen his vision and left Wall Street sooner.

After the meditation, you'll create a Soul's Vision Board to help you leap into your new future. Don't worry—you can revise your vision later as you see fit.

As you work on your vision, remember these important points:

- Visions are uncovered from the heart, not the mind.

- Visions are the gravitational pull to where your soul is leading you.

- Visions don't have to be based in reality.

THE PROBLEM WITH PASSION

When we talk about creating a vision or making a leap toward something new in life, we often talk about the need to connect with our passion to determine what we want to do and where we want to go. But for many people, passion isn't easy to access.

When we spend years avoiding the feeling that we want more than we've settled for, we tend to shut down our passion. We don't want to hear it, so we turn away. Then, we wonder why we feel dulled and depressed.

I recently spoke with my client Shelli Varela, a motivational speaker and creator of the podcast "The Yes Effect," on this subject. "The word and the concept of passion can be super confronting for many people," she told me. "However, if you park 'passion' over here for a second, in front of it is curiosity. And if we give ourselves absolute permission to explore our curiosity without being attached to an outcome, it creates some flow and energy. It allows us to get out of our head. I'm a massive proponent of leading with possibility rather than logic. The only purpose for logic is once you've said yes to a vision, you bring in logic to execute it. But if you lead with possibility, you can rest assured you're pursuing the right vision."

Wise words! If you feel disconnected from your passion, and it feels like a chore finding where it lives inside you, ask for your vision from a place of curiosity and possibility. Let it be whatever it is. Remember: You can always change it later!

 Exercise: Your Soul's Vision and Vision Board

This exercise is in two parts. The first is a meditation, and the second an exercise to create your Soul's Vision Board.

Before starting Part 1, gather magazines that contain beautiful images, as well as a large piece of tag board or poster board, glue, and scissors. You will use these items to create your vision board.

For both Parts 1 and 2, set aside at least an hour of time, although I recommend giving yourself perhaps two hours for both. I know it sounds like a lot, but you deserve to give yourself this time. It's the beginning of a new way of being for you, and you're worth it!

PART 1: YOUR SOUL'S VISION MEDITATION

For the meditation, you will close your eyes for each step and then open them again to read the next portion. Take your time as you move through your vision.

1. Find a quiet, comfortable place to sit by yourself for at least 30 minutes, preferably longer, and turn off all phones. Read steps 1-5 now so that you can follow their directions with your eyes closed. When you're finished, open your eyes and read number 7.

2. Close your eyes, and settle into your seat. Take a few slow, deep breaths, and connect with your inner wisdom. Place your hand over your heart, and feel it beating. Breathe deeply, and with each inhale, fill your chest and abdomen with air. With each exhale, let your body relax even more.

3. Use your breath to drop down deeper, sending the breath to your heart, where your inner wisdom resides. All the answers you seek are readily available from your heart. Even if you feel you have no idea how to find this wisdom, trust that it's there for you and you can access it.

4. Give yourself permission to let go of any thoughts or beliefs that keep you from connecting with your heart's wisdom and uncovering your soul's desires for your future. As you exhale, feel those limiting thoughts and beliefs dissolving with your breath, where they simply disintegrate into the air. You can lower your hand, but stay connected to your heart.

5. Now, imagine yourself sitting in a beautiful garden built to your specifications. In your garden, find a meditation seat that is perfectly formed to hold you. This is a place where you feel completely safe and supported. See your garden vividly in your mind's eye. What does it look like? What colors, sounds, and fragrances surround you? Is there water flowing in a creek or a fountain? Are birds or crickets chirping? (If you aren't a visual person, feel your garden's presence all around you.) Take a deep breath and let the peace of the garden relax you. Take a few more deep breaths as you enjoy this beautiful place. You can return to your garden whenever you feel upset or stressed. Simply close your eyes, say "my garden" to yourself, and breathe deeply. Before continuing, open your eyes, and take notes to help you remember the specifics of your garden.

_____

_____

_____

_____

_____

_____

6. Read this step and number 7 before closing your eyes again. Now that the garden has helped you feel calm and relaxed, imagine that you're returning to your life, but not to your life in current time. You're returning to your life a year from now, after you've created and implemented a new vision for yourself. You don't have to know right now what that vision is. Remember that your vision is the big-picture, feel-good possibility for you. Therefore, imagine the very best scenario you can in vivid detail. Don't be afraid to go big! This is your opportunity to work toward manifesting what you want in your heart of hearts! Breathe into this ideal situation. Connect with whatever activities you're participating in, as well as the people who surround you, the emotions you're feeling, and the sensations you're experiencing. This process is called a "life wheel," in which you envision every aspect of your life.

7. Start by imagining your home life a year from now. Are you living in the same place or a different place? Who is in the home with you? If you're living in the same place, is anything different? If you're living in a new place, what does it look and feel like? How do you feel in your home? Close your eyes, and breathe into your inner wisdom again, centering back down

within yourself. Then, imagine your vision for your life in a year. When you're finished, open your eyes, and take notes on what you envisioned.

_____

_____

_____

_____

_____

_____

8. Read this step and then close your eyes, breathing into your inner wisdom and centering back down within yourself. Imagine your life a year from now in the arena of your family and friends. Are you spending time with different people? Have any of your relationships changed? Which relationships have strengthened or healed? When you're finished with this part of your vision, open your eyes, and take notes on what you envisioned.

_____

_____

_____

_____

_____

_____

9. Read this step and then close your eyes, breathing into your inner wisdom and centering back down within yourself. Imagine your life in the area of intimate relationships in a year. Has anything changed? How do you feel about your intimate relationship? How does your partner make you feel? How do you make them feel? What activities do you share? What values do you share? How is your sex life? What are your beliefs about family and marriage? What are your partner's best qualities? What do you do best together as a couple? When you're finished with this part of your vision, open your eyes, and take notes on what you envisioned.

_____

_____

_____

_____

_____

_____

_____

10. Read this step and then close your eyes, breathing into your inner wisdom and centering back down within yourself. Imagine your life a year from now with regard to your health and wellness. Is anything different for you? Are you eating, sleeping, or exercising differently? Do you feel better physically? When you're finished with this part of your vision, open your eyes, and take notes on what you envisioned.

_____

_____

_____

_____

_____

_____

_____

_____

11. Read this step and then close your eyes, breathing into your inner wisdom and centering back down within yourself. Imagine your life in a year with regard to fun and leisure. What is different from a year ago? How are you spending your leisure and fun time? Have you added more travel? Do you have any new hobbies or pastimes? How do these activities make you feel? When you're finished with this part of your vision, open your eyes, and take notes on what you envisioned.

_____

_____

_____

_____

_____

_____

12. Read this step and then close your eyes, breathing into your inner wisdom and centering back down within yourself. Imagine your work life in a year. Are you working in the same

position, or have you started something new? How does your job make you feel? When you're finished with this part of your vision, open your eyes, and take notes on what you envisioned.

_____

_____

_____

_____

_____

_____

13. Read this step and then close your eyes, breathing into your inner wisdom and centering back down within yourself. Imagine your finances in a year. What do your finances look like? Have they changed in the past year? Have you increased your income or released stress around money? How does it feel to be more at ease financially? When you're finished with this part of your vision, open your eyes, and take notes on what you envisioned.

_____

_____

_____

_____

_____

_____

14. Read this step and then close your eyes, breathing into your inner wisdom and centering back down within yourself. Imagine your spiritual life in a year. Has it expanded from a year ago? Do you feel more centered spiritually? When you're finished with this part of your vision, open your eyes, and take notes on what you envisioned.

_____

_____

_____

_____

_____

_____

_____

15. Read this step and then close your eyes. Allow yourself to see one goal that you could achieve in the next three months. It could be related to any of the areas you've seen in this meditation. When you close your eyes again, breathe into your inner wisdom, center back down within yourself, and imagine the goal you will set to achieve in the next three months. What will be possible for you and your life when you achieve this goal and move closer to your overall vision for your life? How will you feel about yourself if you accomplish this goal? When you're finished with this part of your vision, thank yourself for opening up to this exploration. Roll your head, wiggle your toes and fingers, and shake your shoulders gently to bring your body back to waking consciousness. When you're ready,

open your eyes, and make more notes. Reread the steps of this meditation so that you don't forget any aspect of what you experienced. Of course, write down the goal you have chosen to pursue over the next three months!

_____

_____

_____

_____

PART 2: YOUR SOUL'S VISION BOARD

In this exercise, you'll create your physical vision board. Why make it physical? Your board becomes a roadmap or plan for your vision and putting it in tangible form makes it more real for you. It doesn't allow you to forget it, and it keeps you accountable to your vision. It also sets your intention and puts the Universe on notice that you're serious about working toward your vision. Our minds react strongly to visualizations, and the emotions the visualizations elicit ignite the vibrations in the Universe that manifest our vision.

1. Focus your soul's vision board on the area in which you will accomplish your goal within the next three months. For example, if you want to find a new job, focus your vision board on the area of work.

2. I recommend starting your vision board immediately after the meditation, but if you feel you need more time to determine which leap you want to make, I advise you to take no more than 24 hours. If you struggle to come up with a vision for yourself, ask yourself this question: What would my vision be if I already knew what it was?

3. Gather and thumb through the magazines until you find images that "feel" right for your vision. Don't think about it too much. If you feel drawn to an image in a positive way that seems to represent the vision of the leap you've chosen, cut it out.

4. Search the internet for motivational quotes. You can often find great meme quotes on Pinterest and Instagram. Print quotes you like in a variety of sizes, fonts, and colors, and cut each out.

5. Place all the cut-out images and quotes on your board. Move them around in whatever configuration pleases you and inspires the future you desire. Once you have them placed to your liking, use glue to attach them to the board.

6. Look at your vision board intently, and ask yourself: What two qualities do I need to develop to reach this vision? Do I need more confidence? More courage? More trust in the Universe? Write these qualities down.

_____

_____

_____

_____

7. Then, still looking at your vision board, ask yourself: What two things do I need to let go of to reach this vision? Do I need to let go of fear? A job? A relationship? Write these two things down.

_____

_____

_____

_____

8. When you achieve your vision, what will be different about your life from what it is now?

_____

_____

_____

9. How will you feel about yourself when you achieve your vision?

_____

_____

_____

10. What qualities or things will you have more of? Courage? Happiness? Freedom? Love? Financial success? Write down two or more things you believe you will have once you've seen your vision come to life.

_____

_____

_____

_____

_____

_____

_____

_____

11. Remember that your soul's vision board is a tangible representation of where you're going. It represents your dreams and ideas. If you aren't sure your vision is from your soul, please don't worry about it. There is *no* wrong vision here. Once again, the mere process of creating a vision board will provide you with considerable transformative value.

12. Hang the board where you will see it every day, especially when you first wake up and before you go to sleep. This will help you manifest your vision while you sleep and again set your intention in the morning for the duration of your day.

13. Finally, share your board with someone you trust. It might be your spouse or a close friend, but only share it with someone who will honor it. If that person isn't near you, take a photo of your board with your phone and send it to them. Sharing it with someone else will hold you even more accountable to moving toward your vision, and it will also allow someone else to put their energy toward your intention and manifestation.

ACTION STEPS

As my client Shelli said, logic only comes into play when you begin to devise the goals and action steps you'll take to move toward your vision. You might wonder why you would bring logic into it at all if it's your "soul's" vision. Well, you're still in a physical body, and your soul counts on you taking action!

Think about it: If I had my vision of climbing Kilimanjaro but didn't take action toward it, I would never have gotten there, let alone reached the summit. So in a moment, you're going to choose an action step toward your vision.

Now, I'm sure you've set goals before and not seen them through. We've all done that. How many diets have I started and not finished? When I joined Weight Watchers years ago, I assumed I'd need the program more than once, so I did what I had to do to qualify as a lifetime member to avoid paying the initiation fee again. I suspected I would disappoint myself. What I eventually learned, however, is that trusting my word was one of the most important things I could do to love myself.

How many times have you let yourself down? How many promises or goals got tossed by the wayside? And how often do you let yourself down when you wouldn't dream of doing that to someone else in your life? Yet, somehow, with yourself, it seems to be okay.

We rarely give ourselves the reverence we give others. What would it be like to be as accountable to yourself as you are to other people?

I had a client whose first action step toward a vision of better health was simply to drink more water. When she came back to me the next week, she was upset with herself for making what she had deemed the wrong action step. "I didn't drink the water. I don't like drinking water. It was a stupid action step. I shouldn't have made it," she told me.

I gave her a little tough love and said, "When you go inside and make a decision from your heart, that's what your soul wants from you. Then, when you don't follow through, that's your ego sabotaging you. I don't think we should continue to work together if you can't commit to following through on your action steps because in that case, I can't help you."

Four days later, she called me to say she was in the emergency room with a kidney stone. What did they say to her? "You have to drink more water." Well, you couldn't get a clearer message from the soul than that! As Kelley Kosow has said, "If you don't listen to your body, your body won't listen to you!"[2]

Most of us don't get messages as dramatic as a gall stone, but as we've already talked about, it's important to listen to the messages we do receive!

Of course, I wouldn't want you to beat yourself up for not following through on an action step, but I do strongly encourage you to care enough about yourself to make a strong commitment to your vision. Staying in integrity with your choices equals self-love, pure and simple. When you're able to keep your word to yourself, you reprogram yourself for self-trust. Take it from me, it's enormously powerful! The amount of self-esteem you feel when you follow through on an action is huge. Planning your vision that way can give you a big boost.

For example, four years ago, when I felt a call to move part-time from Aspen, Colorado to California, I had a lot of fears about it. Part of me didn't want to do it. But I could feel that my heart and soul wanted me to make the move, so I took a deep breath and made my way to Sausalito. I rented a place for a month and then tried Mill Valley before I settled in Larkspur. I continue to split my time between the beautiful towns of Larkspur and Aspen.

The first month in California, I didn't know anyone, but I was so proud of myself for having the courage to make the move. I felt like a pioneer woman, and even if it became a blip on the way to my vision, taking that action step increased my self-love many times over. Looking back on it now, I'm so happy I listened to my inner wisdom.

So think of each action step as a mini-goal toward the bigger goal of moving you toward your greater vision and the leap for your bigger life. Remember: the vision is the big picture—the end of your yellow brick road. Each action step is one yellow brick at a time.

Your vision may be unrealistic, somewhat undefined, and not set in a precise timeline. Each action step, on the other hand, should be realistic, well-defined, and in a specific time frame.

THE SMART GOALS MODEL

You've probably heard about SMART goals. They are used in business all the time, but they also apply to this type of self-development work. I recommend this approach when you're creating your action steps toward the goal you've determined to complete over the next three months. Here's what each letter of the acronym means:

- Specific—I like to call these action steps instead of goals because they are smaller steps that will move you toward the larger goal you have specified. You might set a somewhat vague goal of "losing weight" or even "losing ten pounds," but a SMART action step requires that you decide *how* you're going to lose the weight. For example, a specific action step would be to create a precise diet plan or menu so you know what you're going to eat and not eat. Or maybe your action step is to only eat between the hours of 12:00 and 8:00 p.m., which is referred to as intermittent fasting. Be sure to write down each action step with as much clarity and detail as you can!

- Measurable—You should be able to easily know when you have completed each action step. A losing weight action step that limits the periods of the day when you eat to between 12:00 and 8:00 p.m. is easily measured. Whenever you can include numbers, it's easy to tell when you've finished your action. You might have an action step of researching five places you're considering for a move, for instance. When you write down your action step, make it quantifiable so that it's measurable and unmistakable when you have accomplished it!

- Achievable—Unlike your ultimate vision, which may or may not be wholly achievable, your action steps should be 100% achievable. Don't set an action step, for example, that you know you're unlikely to do. If you haven't exercised in years, don't make your action step to exercise an hour a day five days a week. Start with three days maximum for 30 minutes each and work your way up. Set yourself up for success because again, you want to be able to trust your commitment to yourself. In other words, don't choose an action step that dooms you to failure. At the same time, don't let yourself get lazy about an action step you know in your heart is right for you.

- Realistic—Your ultimate vision may not be so realistic, but each action step should be. As I said in the last paragraph, don't set yourself up for failure. Expecting to lose ten pounds in a week or researching 25 new cities in a half hour are unrealistic action steps.

- Time based—Your vision may happen at some undetermined time in the future, but your action steps should be put on the calendar to be completed by a specific date. That is the best way to hold yourself accountable and honor your promise to yourself. Write down exactly when you intend to complete each action step toward your longer goal. We all need deadlines to get things done!

Why is it important to write down each action step toward your goal? Seeing them in print makes them real. Then, share them with one trusted person. Like sharing your vision board with a trusted confidante keeps you accountable, sharing your action steps helps you keep your self-promise to complete each one.

I also recommend setting progressive goals toward your vision. For example, let's say your vision is to open a spa business. A starting action step toward that vision might be to simply research and identify spaces available in the areas that interest you by a specific date. You would write down the viable spaces you find. A secondary action step might be to contact the realtors and make appointments to view the viable spaces by a certain date. The idea is to make small action steps to move you progressively closer to your vision. If you focus too much on the *big* goal of the vision, it might seem overwhelming.

In his book, *The Success Principles,* Jack Canfield suggests implementing "The Rule of 5," in which you take five small action steps toward your vision each day. You might, for example, call five realtors in a day to set up appointments to see the storefronts they're renting.

AVA'S STORY

My client Ava was unhappy in her job, but she didn't know why. After working together, we uncovered that her work didn't allow enough interactions with people. She felt isolated. Her vision was to muster the courage to leave her career. One thing stopping her was the shame she felt for never going to college. It was something she even kept from her children, and it prevented her from getting close to people out of fear that, if they knew, they would judge her. She specifically chose a career that allowed her to work remotely most of the time because she didn't want to get so close to coworkers that they could find out. In this way, she could keep her secret, but her feelings of isolation escalated.

Her first action step was to talk to more people, and when she started to love herself more, she felt brave enough to disclose to others, when appropriate, that she hadn't gone to college. Of course, she discovered that people didn't care, and eventually (along with uncovering other disempowering beliefs), she was able to leave her job and find more fulfilling work.

 ## Exercise: Create an Action Step

How will you decide on your first action step? Simply choose something you believe will lead you toward your vision. Do the best you can; don't worry about it too much. I like to imagine moving toward my vision as pulling back a bow and arrow and shooting toward the bullseye. If each choice I make aligns with the trajectory of that arrow, I have a much better chance of achieving my ultimate vision. And even if I don't, I'm moving in the direction of my greatest learning.

Here's something else that's important to remember: It's okay for your action steps to be "baby steps." What you might deem a "small" step is still a step, and each time you complete a step, no matter how small, you will feel prouder and more confident. Those feelings will fuel you to achieve bigger steps down the road!

It's also okay to make adjustments along the way as you create more action steps toward smaller goals and your ultimate vision. That's part of the process. Seldom is our path to a vision a straight line, so you aren't doing anything wrong if along the way, you veer right and left (or even make a hard turn).

Remember there are two ways up a mountain. One is straight up. It's harder, but quicker and more efficient. The other way is taking the road and going with the switchbacks (zigzag trails). It takes longer, but it still gets you to the top. So each time you deviate from that bow and arrow alignment toward your vision, remind yourself you're on a switchback. You'll still get there as long as you stay on the road.

To determine your first action step, let's go into a mild meditative state again. Read steps 1 and 2 first so that you can keep your eyes closed and remember what to do. When you're finished, open your eyes and read step 3.

1. Close your eyes and take a deep breath, dropping down to your center to access your inner wisdom. You want your action step to come from your heart, not your head, as your heart is free from all the limiting beliefs that rule your ego.

2. Ask for one action step you feel will move you toward your vision.

3. Open your eyes, and write down your action step. Double-check that it fits the SMART criteria! Write it on your computer or device or in a beautiful journal. Make it matter! It's your commitment to yourself. You might choose a first action step to help you develop one of the qualities you wrote down in the vision board exercise. Maybe you want to develop more confidence, so an action step could be to put a sticky note on the bathroom mirror that says, "I am confident." Then, make a commitment to read it out loud every morning and evening for two weeks. That has all the criteria of a SMART action step. If my vision is to find a new relationship, my first step might be to journal in minute detail about the partner I want to manifest. What are their core values, what do they look like, what are their passions, what is their financial status, what activities do we do together, how is our sex life, how do our families mesh, do we travel together, how much time do we spend together, how does this person make me feel, how do I make my partner feel, etc.?

_____

_____

_____

_____

4. Finally, create a commitment statement to solidify what you will do. Write down your vision and action step like the following example below. Complete your action step within the next week if at all possible. Then, continue to create short-term goals and specific action steps using this same process until you achieve your vision.

I, _____, make a commitment to myself to achieve the following vision and action step.

Vision: To have a beautiful romantic relationship.
First Action Step: To make a detailed list *this week* of everything I want in a partner.

Signed: _____

Note that if you're still struggling to come up with a vision and action step, I recommend trying the vision meditation again and focusing on one area you'd like to change in your life. Bear in mind, however, that you might need a personal coach to help you through the process. As they say, nobody gets to the Olympics without a coach. Don't hesitate to ask for help if you need it! (My contact information is in the back of the book if you'd like to reach out to me.)

POINTS TO REMEMBER

The juice is in the journey.

Wherever your soul is pulling you, it's your yellow brick road.

What would it be like to be as accountable to yourself as you are to other people?

Your vision may be unrealistic, somewhat undefined, and not set in a precise timeline. Each action step, on the other hand, should be specific, measurable, achievable, realistic, and completed in a specific time frame.

BIGGER, BETTER, BRAVER MANTRA ACTION

If you struggle to execute your action steps,
say your mantra to yourself

over and over, either aloud or in your mind.
It really does help!

In fact, the more you repeat it to yourself
throughout your day,

the more you will make choices that lead
you toward your vision.

5

PLANNING YOUR LEAP

By failing to prepare, you are preparing to fail.

—Benjamin Franklin

When you decide to climb Mount Kilimanjaro, you don't just hop on a plane to Africa and give it a try. Doing so would not only destroy your slightest chance of success, but you could literally put your life in danger.

Before my Kilimanjaro climb, I planned, planned … and planned some more.

It's true that for most leaps toward something bigger, your life won't be in jeopardy if you don't prepare properly. But planning is *still* a vital part of the process if you're going to set yourself up for a positive outcome.

I know there are lots of tropes out there advising you to leap before you look, and while I appreciate the sentiment, I recommend you plan before you leap! I know people who hated their job so much that they quit with no savings and without another job in place. This is a recipe for disaster. Most of the time, they ended up in dire straits financially or were forced to take an even lesser job ... until they completed the necessary planning. This laissez-faire attitude may work for Peter Pan. But as adults whose actions or *lack* of actions have far-reaching consequences, planning is a necessity.

Before I tackled Kilimanjaro, I conducted a lot of research. I read about others who had climbed the mountain and listened to group calls about the logistics of the climb. I had to learn a myriad of things, compare all kinds of gear, and calculate how much it was all going to cost. I had to determine what I would need for:

- Training before the climb that would gradually prepare me for the arduous task ahead;

- Gear from headlamps to trekking poles to sunscreen to an emergency space blanket to heat packets to UV-blocking sunglasses with side-gussets to a sleeping bag for extreme conditions;

- Clothing that would keep me safe from frostbite, including socks, hats, gloves, jackets, and boots;

- Inoculations;

- Medications;

- First aid;

- Navigation aids;

- Travel insurance;

- Weight limits;

- Snacks and water.

I visited sporting goods stores probably five times before I bought anything, taking a look at what was available and taking notes about what each option would provide and cost.

When it came to training, I had to be particularly careful. Especially with my history of working out too much, it would have been easy to overdo and injure myself or weaken my immune system before I even made the trip. I spent a full six months training and preparing, which included emotional training. Whenever I felt challenged by the preparations, either physically or psychologically, I reminded myself, "If you want to climb Kilimanjaro, you have to start with this." I kept bringing myself back to my vision, as focusing on the goal was the only way I would get it done.

For a physical goal like this, whether it's mountain climbing or a marathon, you have to try all your clothing and gear ahead of time to make sure it's going to work for you. There's a saying that goes, "Nothing new on game day." So I had to sleep at least one night in my sleeping bag and try on all layers of clothing I planned to take. I had to try different drinks and supplements to make sure my stomach handled them well.

Unlike me, Zoe didn't have to *physically* train for her leap, but she still needed a lot of preparation. She had shared a doctor's office with a partner, but when that partnership began to fall apart, Zoe had to figure out how to go into business as a solo physician. First, she had to learn how to create a business plan. This involved research to determine what's required to maintain a doctor's office. "The first thing to do was just to look around me and see what it took—just feet on the ground—to run a medical office," she says.

As Zoe created her plan, she was able to calculate when she would have the financial reserves to break out on her own. She wanted to have enough money put away to survive for a certain period of time, as her solo practice wasn't likely to be immediately profitable. She spoke to other doctors who had done it and found out what they experienced. She asked questions like: *How long did it take them to become profitable? What did they do to turn a profit in that period of time? What hurdles and stumbling blocks should she avoid?*

For example, her research showed her that the month of May is a particularly slow month for doctors in her town. This knowledge helped her make informed decisions about when to open her office. Plus, she could avoid unnecessary panic, knowing a slowdown was just a natural ebb rather than an indication of her future business potential.

Zoe also determined what she needed to learn to be successful. Which tasks was she willing to take on and which would she hire someone else to do? Then, she calculated the costs of that help. Zoe was willing to rent out her beautiful home for many months to gather the resources necessary to sustain her new business as it started out.

Two of the first people she consulted early were a marketing expert and website developer. (Many people in this position would find it helpful to hire a business coach or mentor in the early stages of planning. There is an organization called SCORE (Service Corps of Retired Executives) that offers business counseling with experienced volunteers. There are 63 offices across the U.S. at www.sba.gov/sbdc.)

My friend Adelaide tried a different tactic to get the help she needed for her business. "I realized I knew people with experience that I could consult," she says. "I asked for help and created my own advisory board." Even if someone says "no," many people are willing to help, especially if they can also gain insight from the other people on your board.

What if you don't want to start a new business, but you want to leave your current job? In that case, research the opportunities that are available to you in your field. Do you need additional training? Can you find a mentor through your contacts or SCORE who is already in the field you want to enter? What kind of culture do you want at your new workplace? What kinds of personalities do you want surrounding you day to day? What would be the ideal atmosphere for you? How much do you want to make?

If your desired bigger life leap is to get a divorce, you could interview mediators or lawyers, talk to friends who have gone through a divorce, read books on the subject like *Conscious Uncoupling: 5 Steps to Living Happily Even After* by Katherine Woodward Thomas,[2] and possibly see a therapist or coach—probably before ever bringing it up to your spouse. You need to ask yourself a host of questions: Do you want to try to make the marriage work? If not, what do you want in the divorce settlement? If there are children involved, what would be in their best interests? Where will you live after the divorce? Do you have enough money?

Maybe you don't want to climb Mount Kilimanjaro, but you want to take a trip alone to the Amazon or try something else just for fun. Research the various options and find out what it's like. Watch videos on YouTube and read travel accounts. Like I did, find out the gear, inoculations, and medications you will need.

Whatever change you want to make in your life, *plan it well*, and you'll have a much better chance of success. There's no way to anticipate everything, of course, but with a detailed plan, you're unlikely to be derailed by what you didn't expect. "I think it's important to avoid thinking that you know everything that's going to happen," Zoe says. "I'm anticipating mistakes in hiring, for example. Any employer will tell you that employee management is one of their biggest issues." Adjustments will have to be made, but with your plan in place, you'll deal with fewer mistakes and surprises.

You have already uncovered your vision and set your first action step. So in this chapter, you'll continue with that process, creating a longer-term plan to begin the process of making your vision a reality.

I know there are teachers out there who will tell you it's enough to just have a vision and hold it in your mind's eye, waiting for the Universe to provide it. But in my experience, what separates the successful from the unsuccessful is action.

Have you ever heard of the Law of Diminishing Intent? Let me describe it this way: When an idea first strikes us, the energy around it is high, and the emotions strong. Those emotions and that energy propel us forward. But if we don't translate that energy into action while the iron is hot, the intention starts to diminish until it turns cold and never comes to fruition.

That is why your action steps are so important. They can be small steps, but the idea is to keep moving forward toward your vision. Remember: If the plan is good, the results will be extraordinary!

A CAUTIONARY STORY

Tony had been a lawyer for many years and was becoming increasingly dissatisfied in the profession. Then, things came to a head: "I was trying to collect a major receivable from a client. I was trapped in a case where the court wouldn't let me out, even though we had petitioned to get out for nonpayment of fees," he says.

Around the same time this was happening, he was hired to write a book with a prominent person. The literary agent was certain it would be a "big book." Based on that, he took a leap toward a bigger life and left his law practice.

While he experienced a certain amount of success with that first book, it wasn't big enough to catapult Tony's writing career as he had hoped. "Looking back, it would've been wiser to get educated on how to monetize a writing career," he admits. How could he sell his services for the next book ... and the next? He had no website and had done no marketing, so he wasn't prepared for longevity in his new profession.

By contrast, my friend Ilene was working in an office when she started her writing business as a side hustle. She put up a website and began building her list of clients gradually until she felt she had enough traction to quit her office job. While she couldn't be 100% certain her new business would work, she knew she could go back to an office job, if necessary. She'd never had a problem landing those. Since she planned and was patient, however, she didn't have to work another day for anyone else.

Today, it's nearly 16 years later, and her bigger life has gone in exciting directions she never could have anticipated. Ilene has been able to work with top authors in the publishing industry and increase her income to more than double what she ever made working for others.

 Exercise: Planning Your Leap

In this exercise, you will begin to answer questions to create a plan for your leap.

1. Revisit your action step from Chapter 4. As you create your plan, you will expand on it further.

2. Make a list of what you feel you must research to prepare for your vision. For example, if your vision is to consider a divorce, you might research:

    a. Marriage counselors

    b. Mediators or divorce lawyers

    c. Books on divorce, such as *Conscious Uncoupling* [3] and *Spiritual Divorce* [4]

    d. Friends and acquaintances who have gone through divorce

        i. What worked and what didn't?

        ii. What do they wish they had known in advance?

        iii. What is their biggest regret?

        iv. Who was their greatest resource?

        v. If they had to do it over again, what would they do differently?

    e. Places to live

    f. Schools for the kids in the new prospective neighborhoods

    g. The amount of money you need to survive

_____

_____

_____

_____

_____

_____

_____

_____

3. Make a list of the support team you need to make your vision possible:

    a.   Mediator or divorce lawyer

    b.   Financial advisor or accountant

    c.   Therapist or life coach

    d.   Therapist for the kids

    e.   Real estate broker

_____

_____

_____

_____

_____

_____

_____

4.   Set your action steps for the next week:

    a.   Ask friends for divorce lawyer recommendations

    b.   Research, choose, and order two books on divorce

_____

_____

_____

_____

5. Regularly reflect on your vision and action steps, checking to see if you think you're on the right track. Journal what you feel, and make adjustments as you go along.

6. Set your action steps for the first month:

      a. Meet with financial advisor or accountant

      b. Have first session with therapist or life coach

      c. Decide on areas to move and speak with at least two real estate brokers

      d. Interview three prominent divorce lawyers

_____

_____

_____

_____

_____

_____

_____

_____

7. While you don't have to set action steps beyond the first month right now, you can do so if you wish. You may or may not be prepared to determine those steps right now, so you might need to plan each month as it draws nearer.

8. Find an accountability partner, or at least tell someone of your plan. Write down the names of people you could potentially ask to be your accountability partner.

_____

_____

_____

_____

_____

_____

_____

_____

9. I don't recommend that you move beyond your first initial action steps until you have finished reading the book. You will want the information there before you take any major action, but you can certainly proceed in preliminary steps.

GUARD AGAINST PLANNING FOREVER

Planning for your leap can be very exciting. In that process, you're taking action toward your vision, which naturally brings up feelings of pride. You're in alignment with who you are, doing the work, and walking the talk.

You may be surprised to hear, however, that as you get closer to taking bigger actions, you may feel less excitement and energy about your vision. Why? Because you're close to the big moment of your leap forward, and as a result, your fear has accelerated. This may not feel good, but it isn't bad news! It means you're ready.

If you've executed the steps you set, it's natural to feel more fear as you get closer to making the big change in your life. Visioning and planning can feel wonderful, but the leap is a dance between excitement and overwhelm. After all, that's when you *truly* step outside of your comfort zone.

That's also when you might find yourself stalling. The fear can stop you in your tracks if you aren't careful, and you can plan yourself into a corner, using endless small action steps as an excuse to never take your leap. It's so easy to do, especially if your leap is a truly big step forward for you.

Inevitably, there will come a time when the planning must stop, and the leap itself must take place. Just stay aware that no matter how much planning you've done and how much confidence you've built as a result, you will almost certainly feel afraid when the time comes to actually … *leap*.

So remember …

If you're planning a climb up Mount Kilimanjaro, you'll have to get your plane ticket, get on that plane, show up, and keep going with one foot in front of the other.

If you're traveling to the Amazon, you'll have to get yourself there, first by air and then probably by canoe.

If you're starting a new business, you'll have to put up your shingle, rent a space, and take on your first client or customer.

If you're leaving your job for a new one, you'll have to go on interviews and give notice at your current job.

If you're reentering the dating world, you'll have to put yourself out there, meet someone, and go on your first date.

Here's a reality we all need to face: There's never going to be a perfect time to take your leap toward your bigger, better, braver life. No matter how well you've planned to leave your job, for example, there will never be a perfect time to tell your boss.

So when all the planning is done, it's natural for some resistance to creep back in. Fear will raise its hand and say, "I'm here, and I've just been waiting to stop you and derail your efforts."

So even if you feel excited beyond belief about your vision, you will probably experience fear, resistance, and excuses. Therefore, part of your planning will be emotional in nature. In the next chapters, you'll work through a lot of the material in your unconscious mind that could derail you as you execute your plan. This is why I'm asking you to not take your leap just yet. Right now, you need to stay in the planning stage. The inner work you learn how to do in the next chapters, along with your plan and action steps, will set you up for success when it's time for your leap toward your vision!

Exercise: Cultivate the Qualities You Need

In preparation for the inner work to come in the forthcoming chapters, this exercise focuses on some *emotional* rather than practical planning.

1. What main quality or strength do you need to cultivate in yourself to make your leap a success? For example, you might choose courage, determination, passion, or a sense of purpose.

2. What is one action step you can take right now to cultivate this quality and strength? For example, if you chose courage, you might commit to one small action to step beyond your fear. It could be something like writing your dating profile before you're ready to publish it. Or it could be as simple as visualizing yourself on the vacation you're still afraid to take. If your quality is passion, your one action could be giving yourself pep talks every day to build your emotional connection to your vision.

POINTS TO REMEMBER

I know there are teachers out there who will tell you it's enough to just have a vision and hold it in your mind's eye, waiting for the Universe to provide it. But in my experience, action is what separates the successful from the unsuccessful.

If you've executed the steps you set, it's natural to feel more fear as you get closer to making the big change in your life.

Visioning and planning can feel wonderful, but the leap is a dance between excitement and overwhelm.

BIGGER, BETTER, BRAVER MANTRA ACTION

Spend the next day living as though you have already created your vision

and taken your leap. You have cultivated the qualities you want,

and you ARE a bigger, better, braver version of you.

Do you walk differently? How do you feel?

What's it like to be this new version of you?

6

Understand Faith and Fear

The brave man is not he who does not feel afraid, but he who conquers that fear.

—Nelson Mandela

"When I began seeing Nancy as my coach, I was working in a job I hated," my client Carol says. "I was tortured by thoughts of not being good enough as a businessperson, not having enough, and never getting what I wanted. It was a form of self-torture, and I couldn't find a way out of it. I didn't know where to turn."

Carol was wise to find a coach. She needed an objective viewpoint and tools to help her deal with the fears keeping her stuck.

Her vision had always been to bring more music to the world.

She had worked in the music industry when she was very young but never had the confidence to do what she truly wanted to do—start her own company. "I had to make money to keep my family going," she says. She made little forays into the music business, but when her first attempts were disappointing, she abandoned her dream.

Despite her fears that she wasn't a good businessperson, Carol had been successful in business throughout most of her life. She was the CFO of a company with her husband that brought in $5 million in venture funding. The problem was that it wasn't what she really wanted to do. Curating music to share with the world was her true passion.

Finally, with the help she received from coaching, she took a leap of faith and said, "If I'm going to work, I'm going to do what I love." With that, she devised a plan and put it into motion—even as her fears and insecurities continued to needle away at her.

She already hosted a radio show without pay, so she started scouring the internet to find music she wanted to play on her show. Meanwhile, she attended conferences and found herself on the cutting edge of the music streaming movement.

Then, artists began to contact her and thank her for playing their music. Some of them asked if she would help them with their careers. Before she knew it, she was managing musicians.

Today, in her 60s, Carol runs a company that manages almost 50 music artists and has ten part-time employees. Her next vision is to build her company to 200 clients. One of the fears she had when she started her endeavor was that people wouldn't want to work with someone her age. Like most of her fears, that also proved unfounded.

Carol has had to make some financial sacrifices to make her new business work. "I definitely no longer shop like I used to," she says. But she's also quick to say that it has all been worth it because she loves what she does. "I'm accomplishing something I set out to do. But it's mostly about becoming more *myself*. I am this person who can sign clients. I am this person who has a passion for music and getting artists' music out into the light of the world. That's part of who I am, and that means everything to me."

Again, Carol's fears didn't miraculously go away when she decided to take her leap toward her bigger life. "Today, I still have some of the same anxieties," she says. The difference is that with the help of coaching, she has learned to work *with* her fears and cultivate the courage to go for her vision anyway. Now, she takes action even though her fears are present.

This chapter is designed to help you learn how to do the same.

THE NATURE OF FEAR

Fear keeps many of us stuck because we believe we can't take action unless we get ourselves into a *fearless* state. We believe we have to "get rid" of all our fears before we can move forward. We see others doing what they love, and they appear so courageous and fearless. But nothing could be further from the truth.

They *are* courageous, but they still have lots of fears. As I've said, I was plenty scared when I climbed Mount Kilimanjaro. I was also scared to pick up and move to California. I have been afraid to stay single, travel alone, and even eat dinner out alone. But I've done all of it, sometimes while shaking in my shoes.

Bravery is about feeling the fear, managing those feelings, and moving forward anyway. My client Shelli Varela puts it this way, "Some people will, at all costs, stay in their comfort zone because that feeling of fear has paralyzed them." But it's just that we aren't used to feeling the fear and staying with it while taking action.

As I said early in the book, we must become *comfortable* with the *discomfort* of fear so that we can keep going even as we feel it. We must develop a tolerance for fear because it's always going to be there, especially when we're stepping out of our comfort zone and trying something new. If you remind yourself that you've survived that feeling of fear more times than you can remember, you'll realize you can survive it again.

It's also helpful to remember that fear stands for "False Evidence Appearing Real." Most of the time, our fears are unfounded. As businessman Bob Proctor once said, "Faith and fear both demand you believe in something you cannot see. *You choose.*"[2]

This is why former U.S. President Franklin D. Roosevelt famously said, "The only thing we have to fear is fear itself." Since *what* we fear is usually unlikely, it's often the feeling of fear that we fear the most. Ironic, isn't it? I know we all hate that feeling, so let's try reframing it.

One of my favorite quotes is from Robert Heller, a 19th century businessman, who said, "Fear is excitement without the breath!"[3] So when you're feeling fearful, remember to breathe deeply. All the other physiological responses are the same ones you feel when you're excited. Your heart races, your palms sweat, your energy is high, and you may feel fidgety or tingly.

Bruce Springsteen considers these as signs that he's ready to step out on stage and perform. Others might interpret those same physiological responses as meaning they should run as far away from the stage as possible. This goes to show you how much the mind is involved when we're afraid. So much of it has to do with how we interpret our feelings of fear. The next time you start to say, "I'm afraid," say, "I'm excited" instead. I made this change myself years ago, and it has worked beautifully for me.

Many years ago, I was dating a guy who went to the gym with me. We each got on the treadmill, but after only eight minutes, he stepped off. "Where are you going?" I asked him.

"I broke a sweat, so I'm done."

"What?" I asked him. "When you break a sweat, you're just getting started!"

Many of us *interpret* a sweat—in this case, fear—as meaning we should stop and get rid of that sweat (fear) as fast as possible. Instead, the feeling of fear means we're exactly on the right track—on a path outside of our comfort zone and stretching ourselves to be bigger, better, braver … and happier.

As famed psychologist Abraham Maslow once said, "One can choose to go back toward safety or forward toward growth. Growth must be chosen again and again; fear must be overcome again and again."[4]

If we step beyond our fear and outside our comfort zone—even if it's the tiniest of steps—we begin to grow into who we're capable of being. Often, we're capable of so much more than we realize! But since we haven't been there before, we can't yet imagine it. So we continue to play small, which serves no one. It doesn't serve us, and it doesn't serve society. I believe that self-actualization is our innate responsibility.

Early in his career, my husband at the time would change positions at work and think, "Oh, God, I don't fit into these shoes. I don't know if I can do this." His fears would be activated, as he didn't feel ready or able to accomplish what he set out to do. Then, I would watch him grow into those shoes until his feet were too big for them. Suddenly, he needed bigger shoes, as he was ready for a new challenge that would stretch him even further.

Again, each time, he felt scared, but he pushed himself to accomplish more. We are all capable of our own version of this cycle of stepping into bigger and bigger shoes. But to do that, we have to learn how to keep moving even as our fears are present. Even if our fears are screaming loudly for us to stop.

Exercise: Name Your Fears

In this exercise, you'll discover what fears are standing in your way and prove to yourself how unlikely most of them will ever occur. You will need your journal or a device to record your answers to the questions. It might be helpful to keep your answers to this exercise handy to help you calm your fears when they stop you from reaching toward your vision.

1. Write down whatever comes to mind in response to this question: *If I go after my vision, what am I afraid might happen?*

    Examples: I might fail.

    If I start my own business, I might become bankrupt.

    If I leave my current job, I might hate my new one just as much or even more.

    If I leave my relationship, I might never find anyone else.

    If I travel alone, I might get hurt.

    _____

    _____

    _____

    _____

    _____

    _____

    _____

    _____

2. For each answer you gave in number 1, write down your answer to this question: *If my fear happens, what am I afraid would happen?*

Examples: If I fail, I'm afraid I'll end up hating myself and looking pathetic to everyone.

If I become bankrupt, I'm afraid I'll end up destitute and homeless.

If I hate my new job, I'm afraid I won't be able to find another one I like.

If I never find anyone else to have a relationship with, I'm afraid I won't be able to make it alone.

If I get hurt while traveling alone, I'm afraid I'll die.

_____

_____

_____

_____

_____

_____

_____

_____

3. For each answer you gave in number 2, write down your answer to this question: *What's the likelihood that this fear will come true?*

Examples: I could fail, but I know better than to hate myself. And do I really want someone in my life if they see me as pathetic just because I failed at something I had the courage to try?

It's highly unlikely I will become destitute and homeless, even if I end up bankrupt for a while.

It's possible that I could hate my new job, but that wouldn't be the end of the world.

It's possible that I could end up alone, but is that really worse than being in an unhappy relationship?

It's unlikely that I'll end up hurt or killed if I travel alone. There's no reason to think my chances of dying would be increased simply because I chose to travel somewhere unfamiliar.

_____

_____

_____

_____

_____

_____

_____

_____

4. Once again, for each answer you gave in number 2, write down your answer to this question: *If my biggest fear was to come true, what would I do?*

Examples: If I failed, I would pick myself back up and try something else.

If I became destitute and homeless, I would find a way to get myself out of that situation, and I have people in my life willing to help me. I could even start a crowdfunding campaign.

If I hated my new job, I would work hard to find another I'd like.

If I ended up alone, I would either learn to enjoy my life anyway or keep striving for the relationship I want (or both at the same time).

If I became hurt while traveling alone, I would seek medical attention.

_____

_____

_____

_____

_____

_____

_____

_____

_____

_____

COMMON FEARS

Here are some more fears you may have. If you aren't sure of the fears that hold you back from your vision, this list might be helpful:

I'm afraid of:

Embarrassment.

Being rejected.

Failure.

Losing control.

MAKE FRIENDS WITH YOUR FEARS

Remember my friend Olivia from Chapter 3, who says her inner child gets scared every time she wants to go on a trip? She has a little chat with the little girl inside and calms her fears so that she can travel with less trepidation.

For most of us, fear comes from the inner child. Yet, we treat our fear as an enemy. It does become an obstacle for us, so it's understandable to see it that way. But fear is trying to keep us safe. Sometimes, it does exactly that. It alerts us to real dangers.

Unlike the days of the cave man, fight or flight isn't often necessary for us in modern times. We don't need to fight, and we don't need to flee, even though we react as if we do. Our fears are usually unfounded.

If our fear is coming from our inner child, however, beating ourselves up for being afraid is self-abuse. That is why I think it's better to embrace our fear rather than try to get rid of it (which is impossible) or treat it like an enemy.

So don't try to vanquish your fears. Instead, open your heart to the scared part of yourself. Love and nurture that part of you as you would a small child standing in front of you. The more compassion you have for your fears (and your inner child), the more you will be able to calm them. You won't be able to get rid of your fears entirely, but you can certainly reduce them or ease them by being friendly and understanding toward them.

Making friends with fear will also help you catch when it tries to trick you. Yes, fear is tricky. It sees its job as trying to keep you from harm. The problem is that it believes almost everything is dangerous. So it will masquerade as excuses. Remember those? We talked about them a few chapters back.

You might tell yourself, for example, that you can't do what you truly want because:

> "I'm too tired."—If that's the case, do what you can to get some rest. Often, fear masquerades as laziness, making us tired and keeping us from taking action.

> "I don't know how."—Make a plan to learn how!

> "This is as good as it gets."—This is a limiting belief that we'll address in the next chapter, but it's a form of settling. Someone might stay in a less than satisfactory relationship, for example, saying, "I like the companionship. I really want to have a date every Friday and Saturday night, and I probably won't find anyone else better."

Author and motivational speaker Mel Robbins reduces the "I'm too busy" excuse to a collection of our fears. Fear of change and failure, fear that things won't work out, and fear about what others might think of us. She emphasizes that whenever we hide behind the "too busy" excuse, we avoid taking risks and hard life choices and give fear power over us. She hammers home that it's only when we make time for yourselves and what matters to us that we see we aren't too busy after all and, in fact, have all the time we need.

It's so true. I've seen many people suddenly "find" the time they needed to make their plan and take their leap toward their vision once they made the commitment to do so—no matter what their fear told them.

These are just a few of the many excuses fear might use to keep you playing small. Have you fallen for any of them? I'm sure you have. Most of us have fallen for all of them at some point in our life.

The next time you catch your inner fear voice using one of these excuses, tell your fear gently, "I appreciate your input, but I'm going to take action anyway. It's going to be OK. Life will be too boring— it will be wasted—if I don't do something with these opportunities that are given to me."

Meditation: Making Fear Your Friend

For this meditation, read through all the steps, and then, use your memory to walk yourself through the steps with your eyes closed. Find a quiet, comfortable place to sit by yourself for fifteen to twenty minutes, and turn off all phones.

Before you begin the meditation, locate the photo of yourself as a child you found for the exercise in Chapter 1, as well as the notes you wrote for that exercise. Reread them and keep them in mind as you connect with your inner child during the meditation. Then, spend a few minutes gazing at the photo before you close your eyes and follow these steps.

1. Close your eyes, and settle into your seat. Take a few slow, deep breaths, and connect with your inner wisdom. Place your hand over your heart, and feel it beating. Breathe deeply, and with each inhale, fill your chest and abdomen with air. With each exhale, let your body relax even more.

2. Use your breath to drop down deeper, sending the breath to your heart. Invite your inner child to come sit with you. What does she look like? What's her mood? Look tenderly into her eyes.

3. Ask your inner child if she's willing to have a conversation with you. Be gentle as you speak to this vulnerable part of you. Even if you aren't sure if you've made a connection with your inner child, assume you have.

4. Ask your inner child, "What frightens you most when you think about me reaching for my vision?" You may find that you receive similar answers to the ones you received before, or you may hear something you weren't aware of previously.

5. After hearing your inner child's answer, say something like this in your own words: "I hear and honor your fears. I understand how you feel, and the last thing I want to do is cause you pain. I know that change is scary. It felt safer to just do what other people wanted you to do. You may have learned that it's only safe when you stay quiet and small and do nothing. But know that I'm an adult now, and I *can* take good care of you. It's safe for us to be bigger and try new things. We can take baby steps, but if I move toward my vision, I believe it's going to bring us a great deal of joy. So I'm

asking you to trust me. Take my hand, and let's walk forward together. I love you, and I promise it will be all right."

6.   When you're ready, gently shake your body awake, and open your eyes.

FOSTER FAITH AND CULTIVATE COURAGE

On the other side of fear are *faith* and *courage*. Building your faith and courage will help you quell your fears so that you can keep taking your action steps and move toward your vision.

I have always had a fear of heights and a fear of exposure to falling, for example. I wasn't even comfortable walking on a tree trunk a mere foot above a running creek. Then, a friend of mine visited the Miraval Arizona Resort & Spa, where they have a challenge ropes course to help people overcome their fears. She wanted to go back, so I decided to go with her.

Each day for a week, I had a different rope-climbing experience. The first day, I had to climb up a telephone pole twenty-five feet in the air and then step along a tree trunk that was perpendicular to the pole. I was only allowed to move back to the center and jump down after I had successfully walked across the tree trunk. I was tethered to a rope, so I couldn't get hurt. But my body and mind weren't convinced. I shook like a leaf the whole time yet somehow persevered.

The next day, I had to climb a thirty-five foot pole. At the top was a small red disk about the size of a dinner plate. I had to put my feet one at a time on the disk and will myself, through my fear, to stand up. All the while, the disk was moving. It only stopped once I steadied myself, and only then was I allowed to jump down.

Every day was a new terror, but I loved the experience … even as I also hated it.

I hated it because I was afraid, but I loved it because I knew it was good for me. I can't say it has desensitized me entirely to those kinds of experiences, but it did allow me to do many more things without fear. I did something similar a couple of years later and was still afraid, but knowing I had survived the last time made it much easier to face the challenge. I've been able to call on these experiences to trust my ability to push through my fears. They helped me get through my climb up Kilimanjaro on day four when we scaled the Barranco Wall, a fear-inducing rugged rise straight up almost nine hundred feet.

As you're subduing your fears, do you have to do something as terrifying as a ropes course? No! (Although I recommend it if you're so inclined.) If you decide to take a leap of faith, it doesn't mean that you have to jump out of a plane without a parachute. That isn't a leap of faith; that's suicide. Remember that during my ropes course, I was tethered to a rope that wouldn't allow me to fall. As you cultivate your faith and courage, I want to make one thing clear: Cultivating faith or being courageous doesn't mean you move forward without any sort of safety net. It may be that as you're moving *toward* your vision, you will need to simultaneously move *away* from your current situation. For example, you might start planning your own business while you're still working in a full-time job. There's nothing wrong with that! Keeping to your plan with your safety net in place will help you prevent your fears from overtaking you, and it will also make it easier for you to be successful.

You can build more faith and courage by simply taking your small action steps, too. Even if it's just an inch outside of your comfort zone, each little success will help you feel more confident and courageous, as your faith increases. You'll watch yourself succeed in small increments or step over the obstacles that show up in your way. You'll see yourself getting through each challenge, and you'll watch as the Universe has your back through the process. Remember that things in your life don't happen *to* you, but *for* you, even if they're for your growth through challenge and pain.

Another way to increase your faith is to revisit our discussion about surrender. When you let go of your resistance and surrender to what is, you declare your faith and trust that the Universe will take care of you.

At the same time, watch for messages from the Universe, as we've discussed before. I had an experience like that, which increased my faith a great deal. Shortly after my husband told me he wanted out of our twenty-five year marriage, I went away with a friend to Red Mountain, Utah to practice some self-care. On the last day in the late afternoon, I realized I hadn't gone running the entire week. It was 104 degrees out, however, so I decided to take just a quick half-hour run alone.

I had a portable CD player with me, and I listened to music as I ran. Suddenly, the player stopped. I ceased my run long enough to start to check the batteries, but then, I looked up and felt awestruck as I saw a valley with beautiful red mountains all around me. Just then, out of nowhere, I heard someone behind me loudly say, "You're going to be okay!" I jumped because I had thought I was alone.

I turned around in a circle, looking for the person who had spoken. There was no one anywhere near me as far as the eye could see. Then, suddenly, the CD player began again, even though I hadn't touched the batteries.

Immediately afterwards, I went to a massage appointment and told the therapist what had happened. "That area is an Indian burial ground," she told me. "It's like you were playing Super Mario Brothers and got to the next level."

A few years later, I was reading a book about transitions, and Red Mountain, Utah was named as a place where people often receive messages from the Universe. It also said that we're more open to that kind of experience when we're going through a transition. Even then, I couldn't quite take in the wisdom of the message. I was still holding on to my victimhood. I couldn't let it sink in as real because I hadn't yet fostered my faith enough. Now, after having nurtured my faith and developed my trust in the Universe, I'm able to take in that message. The Universe was trying to tell me that I would be okay. Once I was able to let it in, that experience has increased my faith many times over.

Have you ever felt that kind of love and faith from the Universe? If you have, recall those times whenever you need to feel a stronger sense of faith. Connect with the love within and ask the Universe to shower you with more love. A friend of mine imagines it as the Universe showering her with rose petals or a beam of golden light. If you struggle to connect with that feeling of universal love, take a moment to express gratitude for everything you have in your life from the roof over your head to the hot water in your bathroom. Be grateful for being the unique person you are, and express gratitude to yourself.

Remember this: True courage and faith come from not just feeling confident and strong but from your honest, authentic expression of yourself—even as your fear tells you what you want to do is dangerous. As Debbie Ford said, "The greatest act of courage is to be and own all of who you are—without apology, without excuses, and without masks to cover the truth of you."[5]

RACHEL'S STORY

My client Rachel's story shows that even deep-seated fears can be conquered. When Rachel and I first started working together, she told me her husband was loving and wonderful. After a few weeks of sessions, however, she admitted that the two of them weren't having sex. As we talked about this further, it came out that she suffered from body dysmorphia and an eating disorder. She felt she couldn't have sex with her husband because of how much she hated her body.

I explained to her that if her husband was so loving to her, I was pretty sure her body wasn't an issue for him. He would most certainly want to express his love for her physically. So I gave her an assignment. She was to spend the day thinking of herself as a sexy woman. I asked her to look up videos of pole dancing and try it in the privacy of her own room without looking in the mirror. She was then to text her husband at work and tell him her own version of something like, "I love you and want you, and I need to get laid tonight! So man up and come home ready for action." That way, both of them would spend the whole day anticipating their evening together. When he came home, they made love and had a wonderful time that brought them closer.

This was a huge leap for Rachel, but she was willing to take my advice and do this to move past her body dysmorphia. As a result, she was able to see herself as a sexual being and recognize that her husband's love isn't dependent on how she looks.

Exercise: Your Courage History / Etching

This exercise has three parts. First, you will take an inventory of the times in your life when you've been courageous. Then, you will exercise your courage by making a specific call or sending an email you've wanted to send. Finally, you will learn how to use etching to calm your fears as you simultaneously increase your courage and faith.

PART 1: COURAGE INVENTORY

Review the list of times in your life when you were courageous that you wrote down in Chapter 1. Remember the courage you've already exhibited and add to the list if something more comes to mind.

PART 2: EXERCISE YOUR COURAGE

If there's someone you would love to ask for help or assistance, what's preventing you? Would you call this person if you were more courageous?

What's the worst that could happen? The person would say "no"? If you ask respectfully and graciously, most people will be fine with your request, even if they feel the need to turn you down. But *what if* this person says "yes" and gives you much needed advice?

Set a date to make the call or send the email with your request. Use your mantra "Bigger, Better, Braver" ... and do it!

PART 3: ETCHING

Our fears are often repeated in our minds over and over again until they become "etched" there. This makes them particularly tenacious until we take action to calm them or counteract them with new thoughts.

The etching technique is a way to replace fears and limiting beliefs with positive affirmations. It's an excellent tool that makes affirmation statements more powerful, much like Erin Stutland's movement with mantras technique. Etching supports us in creating new neural pathways (as we discussed in Chapter 3) that help positive affirmations rewire the brain. This can happen at any age! Science has proven that the brain is never too old to change.

1. Choose an affirmation that will counteract one of the deep fears you discovered earlier in the chapter or in the excuses exercise in Chapter 3. *For example, Carol's fear that she isn't good enough could be replaced with "I am talented and capable." Just be sure to keep your affirmation positive. Don't say, for example, "I'm no longer afraid." Instead, say, "I am confident and courageous."* Write down the affirmation you have chosen here:

   _____

   _____

   _____

   _____

   _____

2. Close your eyes, and in your mind's eye, imagine yourself writing your sentence, one letter at a time. You can imagine drawing it in the sky, in sand, or maybe even carving it in clay or on a stone. You can print it or write it in script. You can also close your eyes and envision etching it into your third eye chakra as though you're carving it into your mind.

3. Each time you etch your affirmation in this way, stop and *feel* what it's like to be talented and capable of achieving your vision, or what it's like to feel confident and courageous. Bring on the feeling of fulfillment of your affirmation to the best of your ability.

4. Etch your chosen affirmation ten times at least twice per day, maybe when you get up in the morning and before you go to bed. Of course, if you want to do it more often, please do! The more you do it, the more it will imprint on your mind.

POINTS TO REMEMBER

We have to become *comfortable* with the *discomfort* of fear so we can keep going even as we feel it.

"Fear is excitement without the breath!" —Robert Heller[6]

Open your heart to the scared part of yourself.

Remember that things in your life don't happen *to* you, but *for* you, even if they're for your growth through challenge and pain.

"The greatest act of courage is to be and own all of who you are—without apology, without excuses, and without masks to cover the truth of you." —Debbie Ford[7]

BIGGER, BETTER, BRAVER MANTRA ACTION

Take one small courageous action within the next few days (set a deadline on your calendar).

Maybe you'll eat dinner alone or call someone you've wanted to connect with.

Maybe you'll sign up for a dance or exercise class or attend a networking event.

Maybe you'll tell someone something you've been wanting to say.

Whatever it is, use your Bigger, Better, Braver mantra to propel you into action.

Then, celebrate your bravery!

7

DISCOVER YOUR
UNCONSCIOUS BELIEFS

Life has no limitations, except the ones you make.

—*Les Brown*

When I was five years old, I was playing in the living room while my mother made lunch. It was fire prevention week, so they had been talking about fire a lot in kindergarten. I guess I was a bit fascinated, so when I saw my mom's decorative lighter, I started playing with it. I was sitting at the baby grand piano, and the keys went up in flames in one quick whoosh. My party dress went up in flames next.

I screamed, and my mother ran into the room, quickly throwing me down and rolling me on the floor rug to put out the flames. Her arm was badly burned in the process. I spent a week in the hospital in neck to toe Vaseline bandages and received five injections of medicine a day. Luckily, I had no third-degree burns and was only left with a tiny scar on my thigh. When I returned home, I was afraid to pass the eerily burnt piano in the living room.

Relieved I was alive, my parents didn't punish me. It wasn't until almost fifty years later that the true effects of the event were revealed to me. I was in a car accident, and while I wasn't badly hurt, I was shaken up quite a bit. A few weeks later, my coach took me through a visualization in a beautiful forest filled with the subpersonalities (different parts of me: my inner child, my inner critic, all the various aspects of my personality). Suddenly, I saw a vision of myself when I was five, wearing the dress I wore the day I was playing with the lighter. I was shocked. I hadn't thought much about that day, but the experience in the visualization felt like an exorcism. I realized that the day of the fire was the first time I could have died, and the car accident was the next time I could have died.

"Ask your five-year-old self what she wants you to know," my coach said.

"You aren't safe alone!" my inner child responded. I couldn't believe what I was hearing, but a lot of what I'd experienced in my life began to make sense. I'd had no idea this belief was governing my behavior in my subconscious, but there it was, clear as day.

This belief was logical for a little girl who had been through a traumatic fire, but as an adult, that belief kept me playing small and believing I could never be happy if I was alone. I'd had a boy or man in my life since I was 13 years old and wasn't happy without one. Finally, I understood why.

From the moment I uncovered the belief hidden in the shadows of my unconscious mind, the disempowering belief was gone, as well as the PTSD symptoms I had experienced after the car accident.

Another time in my childhood, my father came home and asked me to go to a farmers' market with him. I was watching TV, so I said I'd rather stay home and finish my show. "What a selfish girl you are!" my mother yelled at me, going into a rant about how my father took time off to spend time with me. I began to cry hysterically and begged my mom to take me in the car to catch up with my dad.

Today, my mother has no memory of this incident, but when she got so upset with me, I felt shamed. So for me, the experience was my initiation into people-pleasing. I concluded from her outburst that I had to always put the people I love first. Their wants and needs should take precedence over my own.

I wasn't aware of these two beliefs, of course, but they took hold in my psyche and became firmly implanted as part of my own personal operating system. They informed my way of being in the world.

Kara Richardson Whitely, the author of *Gorge: My Journey Up Kilimanjaro at 300 Pounds,*[2] has suffered from a history of binge eating. She told me this during our interview: "My earliest memory of binging was when I was nine years old, and my parents were on the verge of divorce," she says. "I would literally hide in the pantry, and the sound of my chewing would drown out their screaming." Food became such a reward or splurge for Kara that when she was home by herself after school, she would raid the kitchen cabinets.

Then, on her 12th birthday, one of her older brothers' friends sexually assaulted her. "He terrified me," she says. "I was frozen in fear." In desperation, she offered him something to eat. "It was such an 'off' moment that it stopped him."

Out of those experiences came the belief that food was her savior, so binging became a way of survival and coping for Kara.

In our coaching sessions, my client David (from Chapter 2) uncovered the memory that when he was a little boy, he was disturbed that his older brother frequently disappointed their parents. He then dedicated his life to trying to impress his parents and others by always being "the good one." As a result, even at age 60, he stayed in a job that made him extremely unhappy. He felt he had to stay there to do the "impressive" thing. When he discovered the belief and finally left the job to follow his passion, he was able to triple his income within six months. He's now happy in a profession he chose for himself.

My client Rob grew up the youngest in a family of five children. His ideas and opinions were usually dismissed when he was a child, so he came to believe his opinions didn't matter. Even as an adult, Rob would stay silent in groups rather than reveal what he thought. When he became aware of this belief, he was able to begin sharing his views at work and in social situations. It changed both his life and career.

Becky was in her 60s when she first came to me. She had just ended a six-year relationship and, much like me, was afraid to be alone. When she traced those feelings back to their origins, she recalled an incident when she was five years old and told her father she was afraid to stay in her bed alone at night. He screamed at her that if she didn't stay quiet, he would lock her in the basement by herself until morning. Not surprisingly, this terrified her, much like my experience after burning myself, and the fear of being alone became part of Becky's operating system. Only when she brought the belief that she wasn't safe alone into her conscious awareness was she able to feel safe enough to be on her own.

These are all examples of how limiting beliefs that develop in childhood affect us throughout adulthood. We can only get past these beliefs when we become aware of them and heal them.

In this chapter, you'll explore how your beliefs prevent you from living your bigger, better life, as well as ways to replace them with new beliefs that can allow you to step out of your comfort zone and take that all-important leap toward your vision.

SHADOW BELIEFS

Founder of analytical psychology C.G. Jung called these limiting beliefs "shadow beliefs" because they live in the shadow of our unconscious until we make them conscious. Even outside of our awareness, however, they are powerful drivers of our behaviors and fears.

Shadow beliefs are usually formed under the age of ten, as we struggle to understand the people around us and our place in the world. As children, we feel so vulnerable that trying to make sense of the world is the only way we feel safe. We're too emotionally immature to comprehend all that is going on around us, but we ascribe meanings to everything. The problem is that the meanings we apply are usually wrong—misinterpretations based on our limited understanding.

Hence, at such a young age, I made the pain of being burned mean something untrue—that I wasn't safe alone *ever.*

Since food spared her another sexual assault, Kara made it mean that food would always save her.

Rob made the dismissal of his ideas as a child mean he would never be safe sharing his opinion.

Debbie Ford said we are "meaning-making machines."[3] When we apply our misinterpreted meanings to our experiences, we create beliefs we think will keep us safe in the scary world of our childhood. Left to operate covertly in our unconscious, however, these beliefs turn us into virtual puppets. We go about our lives behaving and making decisions based on our shadow beliefs, without realizing that the beliefs are pulling our strings.

The more we reinforce these beliefs, the stronger they become. As I've said, neuroscience studies show that repeated actions and thoughts create neural pathways in our brains. So our thoughts can alter our brains. That is why our shadow beliefs are so powerful and why they limit us as adults, preventing us from reaching our full potential and achieving the fulfillment we could if we only learned how to let these beliefs go.

So much of coaching is about exposing and replacing our beliefs with new ones that are empowering and supportive. It never ceases to amaze me what's possible for us when we code our consciousness with new beliefs of our own choice from an adult perspective. I've seen it in myself and all my clients. This is possibly the most life-changing thing we can do.

DO YOU HOLD ANY OF THESE BELIEFS?

Below are some common beliefs that my clients created in childhood.

I'm not good enough.

I need to stay small so no one will see me.

I need to play small so I can stay safe.

I'll never fit in.

Life won't bring me what I want.

This is not my time.

That's for others, not me.

I'm broken.

Food is my savior.

No one will ever love me.

I'm unlovable.

I'll never be successful.

I need to be a good girl.

Boys don't share their feelings.

My feelings aren't important.

I need to control everything so I can be safe.

I need to do everything so people will love me.

My voice isn't important.

If people really knew me, they wouldn't like me.

Luxuries are for others, not me.

People who care about money are shallow.

I'm too old.

It's too late.

You can't make money following your passion.

I can't count on a man; I'll only get hurt.

People aren't to be trusted.

I will never have enough.

 Exercise: Shadow Beliefs Exploration

In this exercise, you will unearth some of your shadow beliefs and work on installing new, more empowering beliefs in your conscious mind. Find a quiet, comfortable place to sit by yourself for fifteen to twenty minutes as you do this exercise.

1. Think about something in your life that frustrates you—something you've been unable to change or achieve. It may be that you've been unable to find a relationship or make the leap you long for toward your vision.

2. What do you tell yourself about this issue that frustrates you?
    What is your negative talk on the subject? Write down what
    you recall telling yourself about it. For example, you might
    hear yourself say, "You'll never find a relationship because
    you're too hard to get along with. Nobody would want to be
    around you all the time. You're just not lovable."

    _____

    _____

    _____

    _____

    _____

    _____

    _____

3. Reread the negative self-talk you wrote in step 2. What
    feelings come up within you as you read these harsh words?
    Close your eyes, and take a deep breath. Try to remember a
    time when you had those same feelings before age ten. What
    were you doing, and who was with you? See if a specific
    incident comes to mind. If not, don't worry. It could be
    that these feelings developed as an ongoing pattern in your
    childhood rather than from one event. Spend several minutes
    scanning your memory before you open your eyes. Then,
    write down what you remembered.

    _____

    _____

_____

_____

_____

_____

_____

_____

4. Here is another way you might unearth a shadow belief: Recall events in your life before age ten that you know were traumatic. What beliefs do you think you have developed as a result of these events? Choose one incident at a time. If you aren't sure of the beliefs you may have created, ask yourself: What beliefs might a child have developed after experiencing a trauma like this? Write down what comes to mind.

_____

_____

_____

_____

_____

_____

_____

_____

5. Choose the belief that holds the most emotional charge for you. How did this belief keep you safe as a child? Write down what comes to mind. Then, take a moment to thank your inner child for working so hard to keep you safe from harm.

_____

_____

_____

_____

_____

_____

_____

6. Now, think about the many times this belief has held you back in your life. What has it cost you in your adulthood? Write down everything you can recall that it has prevented you from achieving or receiving. For example, if you have grown up with the belief that your opinions don't matter, it may have cost you a great deal in your professional life.

_____

_____

_____

_____

_____

_____

7. Although there have been many costs, ask yourself what gifts the belief held for you. My belief of never being alone made me a great partner, and I also had a lot of close girlfriends because I never wanted to be alone. Write down the gifts you've received from your belief.

_____

_____

_____

_____

_____

_____

_____

8. Now that you understand as an adult that your shadow belief no longer serves you, only you have the power to change that belief into a new, empowering one. Write down the new belief you want to imprint on your psyche. Example: *My opinions matter, I have great ideas, and I love sharing them with others.*

_____

_____

_____

_____

_____

_____

9. Finally, decide on an action step to reinforce your new belief. Since I didn't feel safe alone, I decided to stay single for six months and enjoy my alone time. Write down your action step here.

_____

_____

_____

_____

_____

_____

_____

10. You can do this exercise for any number of beliefs you want to unearth and replace.

PROJECTION OF THE SHADOW

Our beliefs also act as a magnetic force. As we project them out into the world, they attract people and situations into our lives that are consistent with those beliefs. This is the simple Law of Attraction—we attract what we focus on.

As our beliefs make us magnetic to *more* of what we believe to be true, they become self-fulfilling prophecies. Let's say a woman's father cheated on her mother, so she grew up to believe all men are dishonest. As she projects this shadow belief out into the world, she's likely to attract men who are dishonest. If she does attract someone who is honest, she will look at him through the lens of her shadow belief and interpret his behavior as dishonest. These experiences only further prove to her that her belief is accurate, but it's simply a result of projection. If she can create a new belief about men, she has the potential to attract ones who are trustworthy and to see them as such.

Like many of us, my friend Janice grew up putting herself down in her own head. As she projected negative beliefs about herself out into the world, she attracted mean girls and women who also put her down. When she experienced coaching and began to develop her self-esteem, she finally took a stand and told one of those women that the putdowns were unacceptable. After that, she no longer projected negativity about herself outward and stopped attracting "mean girls" into her life.

Everyone we meet is a mirror of what's going on in our unconscious mind—our shadow. In fact, C.G. Jung said that whenever someone else's behavior upsets us, it means we have disowned a part of ourselves that the other person's behavior displays.

Let me explain it this way: When we're babies, we embrace all parts of ourselves. Then, others show disappointment in one of our qualities or behaviors, and this leads us to believe that some parts of us may not be acceptable. So in an effort to be loved, we disown those parts and try to stop exhibiting those qualities or behaviors.

Debbie Ford used to say we start out with, say, one hundred qualities. As we grow into adults, we close the door on perhaps seventy we deem unacceptable. This leaves us with thirty of our original one hundred parts that we believe are okay for us to express.

One of my parts that I disowned was "laziness." I carried a belief that laziness was unacceptable. Therefore, it was no surprise when I attracted a lazy man into my life, and it became a huge issue for us. When I learned about disowned qualities, I realized I only judged him harshly because of my own shadow belief about laziness. I judged him because I had disowned that part of myself. Since his behavior upset me—"triggered" that disowned belief inside of me—it was my job to bring that belief into awareness and reintegrate the disowned quality.

As we discover our disowned selves, we can be honest with ourselves about where we exhibit that quality or behavior. At first, it was hard for me to see when I had ever been lazy. After all, I tend to be a workaholic and an over-exerciser. But as I examined further, I realized that I'm lazy in some ways. If I forget something in my car, for instance, I almost never go back for it. I hate parking far away from where I'm going. If something doesn't contain the name "exercise," I can be extremely lazy.

The next step was to look at the *gift* of being lazy. Every quality we deem unacceptable has a positive side. Embracing laziness meant I could learn to relax and give my body a rest. I could balance out my workaholism. I could binge-watch a Netflix series.

I'm also a punctual person who got triggered by people who are late. My ex-husband was usually late, as was my oldest son. My father used to say that if the house was on fire, my son would get his ass burnt. After my marriage, I briefly dated a man who was almost always late. It blew up into a big argument one night because he was late to his own work function, which forced me to take over as hostess even though I didn't know any of his guests. When I worked on this trigger, I realized that for me, the disowned quality was "disrespectful." While lateness could be the result of different qualities, "disrespectful" was the one that triggered me the most. So I had to think about when I'm disrespectful.

I had to admit that I'm disrespectful when I look at my phone in a meeting or talk to the person next to me during a class. To reintegrate that quality, I needed to find the gift in it. Again, the gift could be different for someone else, but for me, it meant I could consider doing what I wanted to do regardless of the other person's needs. Bringing this back to my friend who was always late, he took care of everything he wanted to do before he showed up to meet other people. This is what prevented him from being on time.

When I was able to reintegrate this quality within myself, I (a) didn't get as upset when people were late; (b) modified my behavior when meeting them, rather than try to change them, so I wouldn't show up early and have to wait around; (c) stopped freaking out if something made me a little late; and (d) stopped attracting partners who were late. Reintegrating that quality meant I no longer needed a man who wasn't punctual to mirror back to me my disowned self.

The point is that we all have qualities on both ends of the spectrum. We become more balanced when we own a little bit of both. It isn't necessary to make a quality wrong because there's a time and place for all qualities and behaviors.

Think of it using this metaphor: You're out in the world like a robot with electrical wires extending from all areas of your body. Each wire represents a quality you either own or disown. The qualities you *own* have rubber tips on them, while the qualities you *disown* do not. The qualities without rubber tips are like live wires, and when you encounter someone with that quality, you receive a little shock that triggers you. Then, you become agitated and argumentative. You might overreact and blame the other person for what you're feeling.

If you use coaching to reintegrate these disowned qualities, you essentially add that rubber tip to the live wires so that you are no longer triggered by them in others.

By owning more of who we are, we become less reactive and set ourselves up for a successful leap toward our vision. This is not about making ourselves wrong. It's about emotional education and becoming more whole.

When we project our shadow beliefs out onto others, we also create meanings about them. We come to inaccurate conclusions and make assumptions that have to do with our own history, not the other person. Since this happens outside of our conscious awareness, it's a robotic, autopilot behavior.

Projecting our shadow beliefs onto others causes us to make snap judgments about them. When I climbed Kilimanjaro, there was a 30-something woman in my group who decided from the moment she saw me that she didn't like me. We had never spoken to each other, so to this day, I have no idea why she felt this way. She bullied me throughout the trip, trying to push me out of the way and ignoring me when I tried to speak to her. Obviously, she made a snap judgment about me and projected negative feelings about herself onto me.

In the past, I would have allowed her behavior to ruin my trip, but with the awareness I learned in coaching, I was able to feel sad for her. I knew it was her own self-hatred and insecurity that she was expressing. Whatever she felt, it had nothing to do with me.

This is the pain that the projection of our shadow can cause in our lives. If we stay unaware of this powerful unconscious force, we will find it difficult to live the fullest possible life. Let's do an exercise to learn how to take back some of these projections.

 Exercise: Take Back Your Projections

In this exercise, you will look at situations in your life in which you have projected your shadow.

1. Think of a recent incident in which someone upset you. What did they do that caused you to feel angry or hurt? Perhaps someone gave you unsolicited advice or asked you a personal question you felt was inappropriate.

   _____

   _____

   _____

_____

_____

2. What possible qualities did this person display when they upset you? If they offered unsolicited advice, for example, maybe the quality was condescension, judgment, or being a "know-it-all." If they asked a personal question, perhaps the quality was nosiness or meddlesomeness. If you can think of several qualities, write down all of them. Then, choose the quality that you dislike the most. Which one would you least want someone to say about you? This is an example of a disowned self.

_____

_____

_____

_____

_____

_____

_____

3. Now, ask yourself: *When have I displayed this quality?* This might be difficult for you, as you don't want to think of yourself as having this quality. It's likely that you display it in a much subtler way than the person who upset you, so you may have to think hard to find it in your own behavior. It may, in fact, look entirely different from the person's behavior that

upset you. For example, if someone is abusive, and you can't come up with any way you would be or have been abusive, ask yourself how you might be abusing yourself.

_____

_____

_____

_____

_____

_____

_____

_____

4. Lastly, think about the gift in the quality or behavior. The positive aspect of condescension might be an ability to explain something in a way that's easily understood. For the person who is being condescending, feeling superior certainly seems like a gift. Here are more examples: The positive aspect of judgment might be the ability to be discerning and maintain high standards. Meddling can be helpful when it assists someone in need, and for the person who meddles, the behavior satisfies their curiosity. Sometimes, the gift of a quality is that you've hidden it so well, you become the exact opposite. If you had a judgmental parent, for instance, you might have developed a laissez-faire attitude so no one would ever call you judgmental. But you might still be judgmental of yourself. As you integrate the part of you that's judgmental, you'll be less likely to attract judgmental people into your life. But you may still have to set boundaries with others you feel

are overly judgmental. That's the case with me and laziness. I now see where I'm lazy in my life, but I still don't want a relationship with a lazy man. Now that I've owned that quality in myself, however, I haven't attracted another lazy man into my life.

_____

_____

_____

_____

_____

_____

_____

5. Now, close your eyes, and picture the quality you pinpointed in the exercise as a wire extending from your body. Imagine you're adding a rubber tip to it so that you will no longer be triggered when someone displays this quality or behavior.

6. The next time someone behaves in this way, take a deep breath, and remind yourself that you also have this quality in you. Imagine yourself owning this quality within yourself, reintegrating it as an accepted part of you.

Remember: Our shadow beliefs deter and limit us. Then, when we try to create our bigger life, we create obstacles instead as we project those beliefs into the world and attract what we don't want. They derail us and cause us to lose heart. If you have a belief you aren't good enough and don't have what it takes to accomplish what you want, working toward your leap will be an uphill battle.

The more emotionally whole we become, the better we can take the actions in our life that lead to fulfillment and joy.

TAPPING (EFT)

Tapping or EFT (Emotional Freedom Technique) combines Chinese acupressure with modern psychology. It alters your brain, energy systems, and body all at once. During this practice, you will use your fingertips to literally tap on specific acupuncture points on your body, as you focus on a certain emotion or traumatic memory. The process helps you focus on and activate your body's natural healing capabilities and creates new neural pathways to retrain your brain to think differently.

You can choose a specific shadow belief to focus on and create an entire dialogue based on that. You can use the one I've provided or write down your own once you get the hang of tapping. I have provided a video download of this tapping sequence for your convenience: https://nancypickardlifecoach.com/bigger-better-braver-resources/

1. *Identify the Issue*—Name the specific problem or emotion you want to target with EFT. The goal is to focus on only one issue at a time for the greatest effect. For example, in this case, you might focus on a shadow belief or disowned quality.

2. *Create a Reminder Phrase*—Create a short phrase that helps you refer to the problem or memory in a specific way by giving it a title. This helps you stay focused on the problem during the rest of the process.

3. *Rate the Issue*—Using an "intensity scale" ranging from 1-10 (with 1 as the least significant and 10 the most), determine how significant the problem is to you.

4. *Set Up Your Affirmation*—Come up with a self-affirming phrase that helps you feel powerful in response to the issue. The basic structure of positive affirmations is "Even though I feel X (fill in the problem or emotion you're dealing with), I'm willing to love and accept myself." For example, you might say, "Even though I have a shadow belief that I'm stupid, I'm willing to deeply and completely accept that I'm intelligent." While you repeat your affirmation, use your dominant hand to tap on the fleshy part of your palm under your thumb of your non-dominant hand.

5. *Perform the Tapping Sequence*—During a tapping sequence, you will tap on nine key meridian points. Use two fingers—usually the middle and index finger—applying constant, gentle, yet firm taps as you say the phrases out loud. The meridian points include (in this order): karate chop to the fleshy pad under your thumb, the top of your eyebrows, the sides of your eyes, under your eyes, under your nose, in the crease of your chin, on your collarbone, in your armpit, and on the top of your head.

6. *Tune in for Re-Rating*—Tune in to how you feel about the tapping session, rating the problem once again on a scale from 1-10.

7. *Repeat the Process*—If you still feel stuck, create a new positive affirmation, and repeat the process using the new line.

On the next page are two scripts of the videos that you can access from my website. Depending on time, or need, you can choose the shorter version or the longer version.

SHORTER VERSION

(Do the karate chop side of thumb as you say)
Even though I feel unworthy, life is not how I want it, I love and accept myself. My life feels so hard, and I look at everyone else and think they are happier.

(Top of the eyebrow)
Everyone is happier and doing the things I want to be doing. Life is so hard for me. Everything goes wrong. I am always afraid, and I feel guilty for not having a better life. I love and accept myself.

(Side of the eye)
I choose to release what is holding me back and surrender even deeper. I am clearing any resistance to having what I want. I give up all excuses.

(Under the eye)
I release all my beliefs that I am not allowed to be happy.
I release all my beliefs that I don't deserve love.
I release all beliefs that I was abandoned or unloved, and I love myself completely.

(Under the nose)
I release my fear of change, and I release holding on to the past.
I forgive myself for believing all my excuses for why I couldn't get what I wanted.

(Crease of the chin)
I release all beliefs that I need to hide my feelings.
I release all beliefs that I am not confident and courageous, and I love and accept myself. I release believing the limitations of my negative self-talk.

(Collar bone)

I love and accept myself. Wealth wants me, and I choose to accept it. Love wants me, and I choose to accept it. Health wants me, and I choose to accept it. Success wants me, and I choose to accept it.

(Under the armpit)

I know the Universe has my back, and everything I want is coming to me. I trust that everything is on its way to me.

(Top of the head)

Thank you, Universe, for all the gifts you are bringing me and have already brought me. I thank you, and I love and accept myself. I am grateful for all the gifts and lessons life is teaching me. *My heart is bursting with gratitude. I feel so held by the Universe.*

Now breathe it in.

See how you feel. If you don't feel markedly better, repeat another cycle, and check in with yourself again. Keep doing it until you feel a shift in your emotion

LONGER VERSION

(Do the karate chop on the side of the thumb as you say)

Even though I am unhappy, and life is not the way I want it,

I know that what I want wants me, and I choose to love and accept myself.

I think everyone is happier than I am. I believe the lives of those around me are fuller, and my life is not the way I want it.

(Top of the eyebrow)

What I choose to know is that what I want, wants me.

I choose to release what is holding me back and surrender even deeper.

(Side of the eye)
I am clearing any resistance to having what I want.
I give up all excuses. I trust in the Universe.

(Under the eye)
What I really want is already available. I am clearing any beliefs that I am not good enough. I am clearing any beliefs that I can't have this. I am clearing any beliefs that I won't be successful. I am open to the possibility that what I want, really wants me.

(Under the nose)
I am clearing any fear about getting what I want.
It is safe to get what I want.
Wealth wants me, and I choose to accept it. Love wants me, and I choose to accept it. Health wants me, and I choose to accept it. Success wants me, and I choose to accept it. My vision for my future wants me, and I choose to accept it.

(Crease of the chin)
I know everything happens for a reason. This is my time.
I forgive myself for not listening to my intuition.
I forgive myself for staying silent when I should have spoken up.
I forgive myself for saying yes when I wanted to say no.

(Collar bone)
I forgive myself for depriving or punishing myself.
I forgive myself for not loving myself.
I forgive myself for not knowing my worth. I love and accept myself fully.

I release all my fear and resistance. I forgive myself for my past.
I release all my disempowering beliefs.
I release all my sabotaging habits.

(Underneath the armpit)
I release all addictions.
I release all my fear and resistance that keeps me stuck.
I release all my fear and resistance to follow my heart.
I release all my beliefs that I am not confident or courageous.

(Top of the head)
I forgive myself for all the times I didn't play all out.
I forgive myself for all the times I played small and didn't trust myself.
I forgive myself for all the times I didn't remember the Universe had my back.
I love and accept myself.

(Karate chop)
I release my decision to block my power.
I release all beliefs that I need to hide my feelings.
I release all my beliefs that my voice is not important.

(Top of the eyebrow)
I release all my beliefs that I am not allowed to be happy.
I release all my beliefs that I don't deserve love.
I release all beliefs that I was abandoned or unloved.
I release believing the limitations of my negative self-talk.
I love myself completely.

(Side of the eye)
I release my fear of change. I release holding on to the past.
I forgive myself for believing all my excuses.

(Under the eye)
I am saying thank you, Universe, right now.

(Under the nose)
Thank you for the gifts you are giving me.

(Crease of the chin)
Thank you, Universe, for always having my back.
I am allowing myself to feel grateful right now.

(Collar bone)
I am already connected to what I want. I allow myself to feel deeply grateful.
I am whole.

(Under the armpit)
My heart is bursting with gratitude. I feel held by the Universe. I love and accept myself.

(Top of the head)
The gifts from the Universe just keep coming. Thank you, thank you, thank you!

Now breathe it in.

See how you feel. If you don't feel markedly better, repeat another cycle, and check in with yourself again. Keep doing it until you feel a shift in your emotions.

POINTS TO REMEMBER

Our shadow beliefs are usually formed under age ten, as we struggle to understand the people around us and our place in the world.

It never ceases to amaze me what's possible for us when we code our consciousness with new beliefs of our own choice from an adult perspective.

As our beliefs make us magnetic to *more* of what we believe to be true, they become self-fulfilling prophecies.

Everyone we meet is a mirror of what's going on in our subconscious mind—our shadow.

The more emotionally whole we become, the better able we are to take actions that lead to fulfillment and joy.

BIGGER, BETTER, BRAVER MANTRA ACTION

Now that you've had some experience walking through a day as your

Bigger, Better, Braver self, spend this day repeating the mantra as many times as possible.

How many ways can the mantra incite you to try harder?

8

EXPLORE THE UNCONSCIOUS COMMITMENTS YOU'VE MADE

To transcend limitations and form positive new patterns of life based on who you know you can be rather than who you were yesterday, you must give up the modes of thinking, feeling and behaving that only keep you chained to your past.

—Debbie Ford

"My parents were both deceased by the time I was 16," Ruth says, "so I was on my own at a very young age. My father died in an airplane crash when I was 13 years old. My mother passed away when I was 16, two months before my 17th birthday." Despite the tragedies she experienced, the adults in Ruth's extended family were unmoved and refused to take her in. Instead, they said, "You're old enough to be on your own" and left her to her own devices without the guidance of an adult. At 16, she was forced to try to survive on her own.

All Ruth's aunt was willing to do was cosign on a lease for an apartment, and Ruth then had to work two jobs while attending GED classes in the evening. She couldn't afford a car, so she walked home late at night from her second job.

Feeling abandoned by every adult in her life, Ruth developed a deep shadow belief that she was a "disposable" person. She knew intellectually, of course, that her parents didn't choose to leave her, but the feelings of abandonment were still there. Then, when her aunts and uncles were unwilling to help her, the abandonment was exacerbated a hundred-fold.

To this day, Ruth has difficulty making friends. She has to push herself through the fear that inevitably comes up when she meets someone she would like to get to know better. Her inner child immediately becomes afraid of the possibility of abandonment.

At the same time that Ruth developed her shadow belief about being disposable, she made a commitment to herself—a promise in her unconscious mind that she wouldn't let herself get too close to anyone. That way, if someone rejected her, it wouldn't hurt as much.

Through coaching, she has become aware of this unconscious commitment to avoid hurt, so she is now able to gently lead her inner child through the fear and open herself up in relationships when she chooses. But it hasn't been easy.

Unconscious commitments like these are promises we make to ourselves to spare ourselves pain and abandonment. We aren't consciously aware of them, but they still drive us in our lives and often prevent us from creating what we want.

Remember the story about the fire when I was five years old? My then nine-year-old sister came home from school for lunch that day as it was happening, so she was rushed off to the hospital with the rest of us. By 5:00, she began to cry because she had never gotten her lunch and was hungry after so many hours without food. It was a natural response for a child, of course, and her tears were no doubt intensified by her fears about what would happen to me. She could clearly see how frightened our parents were, and for all she knew, her little sister was about to die. It must have been terrifying for her.

On the one hand, she was hungry and couldn't help but respond to her body's needs. On the other hand, she felt guilty that her tears caused our parents more stress. She was old enough to internalize the feeling that she "shouldn't" cry or ask for anything while her sister was in the hospital. But she wasn't remotely equipped to make sense out of the inner conflict between her hunger and her guilt.

Somewhere in all that confusion of fear, emotion, guilt, and physical hunger, my sister came to believe that she had not only been home when I played with the lighter and started the fire, but that she either suggested I play with it or, at the very least, didn't stop me from playing with it. This false memory plagued my sister her entire life until her 60s, when she finally sought coaching and discovered how much that event had affected her actions and reactions through the years. We were able to set the record straight that she wasn't present when the fire started, but the damage had already been done for many years. This is the kind of unconscious "meaning-making" that our young psyches can concoct, especially when we go through something traumatic.

Coaching also unearthed an unconscious commitment that my sister made that day when I was in the hospital—a commitment that laid the foundation for weight issues throughout her life. Because her hunger was so tied up with the trauma of the day, including her worries about my safety and worries about being a bad person for crying over her hunger, she vowed to never allow herself to be hungry again. This started a fear of hunger that led her to overeat. No matter how hard she tried or how many times she dieted, her underlying commitment to never go hungry was the commitment she adhered to. Amazing, isn't it, what our young minds do to make sense of the events of our lives?

Every one of my clients has unconscious commitments that have derailed their lives in some way. I could list dozens of them. Here are two:

Sam became an excellent tennis player when he was a boy, but when he failed at a big tournament, he felt terrible shame. His friends even laughed at him. So he made the unconscious commitment then and there to avoid being seen so that he wouldn't be shamed again. He never entered another tournament and held himself back in all areas of his life in order to hide and avoid humiliation.

Molly grew up in a chaotic household with a narcissistic mother. Since she felt so out of control in her life, Molly made an unconscious commitment to maintain control over the one thing she could—her body—a commitment that led to anorexia.

If you've told yourself you want something, but you've struggled—perhaps for years—to make it happen, I'd be willing to bet that an unconscious commitment is in the way. In this chapter, you'll explore these unconscious commitments that may be holding you back from taking your leap and living your biggest life. Then, you'll make new, *conscious* commitments that will give you the freedom to design the bigger, better, braver life of your choice.

HOW UNCONSCIOUS COMMITMENTS WORK

Just like the shadow beliefs that form as a result of an emotionally charged experience, we make these commitments to either cope with painful situations or to avoid pain altogether. For example, let's say when you were a young child, you made a presentation in class at school. One of your classmates laughed and shouted, "That's stupid!" The other kid may have simply felt the need to put you down to feel better about himself. But his comment stung so much that you created an unconscious commitment to stay quiet for the rest of your life and avoid being seen as stupid ever again. In this way, our unconscious commitments affect our daily behaviors, as well as the choices we make.

This commitment may have also offered you a gift, however, because perhaps it caused you to spend your life proving to the world you aren't stupid, helping you to excel. Yet, deep inside, your inner child still believes you're stupid, so you only do what you know you do well. This cuts you off from trying anything new and challenging. The fear of being "found out" as "stupid" is always a driver in your decision-making process.

What if, as an adult, you have a desire to become a motivational speaker, but have the unconscious commitment to stay quiet? How can you negotiate the desire to get up on stage with the desire to stay silent? You aren't sure you can excel right away, so chances are, you'll find a way to derail your efforts to become a speaker. This is because you're more committed to staying quiet than getting on stage. The only way to make your dream a reality is to bring your unconscious commitment to consciousness and create a new, *conscious* commitment that will serve you better in adulthood.

I knew a woman named Rhonda with an extremely controlling father who constantly told her she was making the wrong choices. As a result, she grew up with the belief that she didn't make sound decisions. To feel safer, she made an unconscious commitment to let others make decisions for her whenever possible. When she was forced to make a choice on her own, she went to extreme lengths to ensure her choice was a good one. This meant going over the options repeatedly, checking and rechecking every detail. Making a jump and living a big life eluded her because those kinds of decisions were too frightening. Rhonda avoided anything she deemed too risky, and her unconscious commitment kept her playing small ... and kept her unhappy ... throughout her life.

Valerie is another example of someone with an unconscious commitment that stood in the way of what she wanted. Her mother was as beautiful as a model but spent her life as a stay-at-home mom. Valerie always believed her mom didn't fulfill her potential and was trapped in their family of six kids. Her mother may or may not have felt that way, but it was how Valerie interpreted the situation. Valerie made the unconscious commitment to never let herself become trapped like her mom.

As an adult, she wanted a romantic partnership very much, but she couldn't figure out why she could never sustain a relationship. Why was she still single? She wasn't able to heal until she started coaching and discovered her unconscious commitment to avoid relationship entrapment like she believed her mom had endured.

Here's the truth: We always get exactly what we're most committed to, regardless of what we *think* or *say* we want. If our unconscious commitment is stronger than our desire as an adult, it's exactly what we'll get. So even though Valerie believed she was committed to attracting a relationship, she was more committed to avoiding entrapment. This is how our unconscious commitments hold us back in life.

The commitments we make when we're very young usually hold on for dear life in the psyche, no matter how much we change and grow over the years. As long as those commitments are unconscious, they will wreak havoc.

For example, when I developed the belief at age five that I wasn't safe alone, I created an unconscious commitment to make sure I was never alone again. From the outside looking in, this seemed like a great idea. Throughout my school years, I was popular and had a multitude of friends. By the time I became a teenager, I always had a boyfriend, and I was a great girlfriend because I went out of my way to avoid losing my boyfriends. If I did lose one, I made sure I quickly replaced him with another.

Then, I got married young and felt safe because I had fulfilled my unconscious commitment to myself. I wasn't alone ... until my husband decided he wanted a divorce. Suddenly, my world was turned upside down. Circumstances forced me to break my commitment to myself, and I was alone for the first time.

Right after my divorce, I was financially secure, healthy, and still young enough to enjoy life, but I was stuck in the victimhood that my shadow belief and unconscious commitment had created. I was alone, which didn't feel safe, so my focus was on finding another relationship as fast as possible. I *needed* to rectify my aloneness to maintain my commitment to myself.

If it weren't for my shadow belief and unconscious commitment, I could have lived a much bigger life during that period. I could have traveled on my own and tried new things without focusing on my fear of being alone. Instead, I was stuck and didn't enjoy my life as I could have.

At the same time that I had the childhood unconscious commitment to never be alone, I developed a new unconscious commitment after my divorce to keep my heart safe. These two commitments—one made in childhood and one in adulthood—were in direct opposition to each other. I believed I couldn't keep my heart safe unless I was alone, yet I didn't feel safe alone. I was between a rock and a hard place.

It was only when I brought these commitments into consciousness through coaching that I was able to feel safe being alone. I could even enjoy my time by myself. I could also feel safe allowing my heart to be engaged in a relationship. Rather than seek a relationship out of a place of fear, I could choose one that I truly wanted because I no longer felt threatened by the possibility of aloneness.

Unconscious commitments are made for the instant gratification of soothing a wound in the moment. When we look at the commitment consciously and logically, we see that the long-term gratification that's possible *without* the commitment is better for us. For example, someone who wants to lose weight may be more committed to the short-term gratification of eating what they want than the long-term gratification of feeling healthier and looking better. The short-term gratification of overeating no doubt soothes a wound.

In another example, the short-term gratification is the avoidance of discomfort and fear. If someone who has grown up afraid of looking stupid wants to become a speaker, for instance, they may have to risk looking stupid to fulfill their dream of speaking on stage. They will have to endure short-term discomfort to achieve the long-term gratification of their dream.

So to live life on our own terms as adults, we must become aware of the unconscious commitments hiding in our psyche. Let's try an exercise to bring some of yours into your consciousness. While this exercise can be powerful and enlightening, you may find it easier to uncover these commitments with the help of a coach.

Exercise: Uncover Your Unconscious Commitments

In this exercise, you will contemplate possible unconscious commitments that are holding you back from taking your leap and creating your bigger life. Then, you will create a new, conscious commitment to replace the old one.

1. Close your eyes, take a deep breath, and as you exhale, quiet your mind to the best of your ability. Take two more deep breaths, and continue to slow down your breathing and quiet your mind.

2. Ask yourself: *Where in my life am I not getting what I want?* Maybe you want a romantic relationship but have been unable

to sustain one. You might want to start your own business, but you never seem to be able to get started. Financial security may always elude you. Or your efforts thus far have fallen flat without success. Write down 1-3 things in your life that you want but have struggled to create.

_____

_____

_____

_____

_____

3. Now, ask yourself: *What are some possible unconscious commitments that might have gotten in the way of what I want?* Write them down. For example, if you want a relationship, potential unconscious commitments could be:

> *I'm committed to making sure I'm never rejected, so I don't let anyone get too close to me.*

> *I'm committed to staying independent and doing what I want in life, so I can't allow anyone else's desires to interfere with my own.*

> *I'm committed to staying single because I don't believe anyone could ever love me.*

_____

_____

_____

_____

4. As you've seen, shadow beliefs and unconscious commitments often go hand-in-hand. If you're finding it difficult to think of your unconscious commitments, it might help to review some of the shadow beliefs that you unearthed during the exercise in the last chapter.

5. Review the potential unconscious commitments you wrote down. Do any of these have an emotional charge for you? Which one *feels* the most right? If none feel quite right, come back to this exercise later and try it again, or work with a coach to help you find the unconscious commitment that's hindering your development. For now, however, work with the one that feels closest to correct. Even if it isn't exactly right, it probably contains elements of truth. Write the unconscious commitment below.

_____

_____

_____

_____

_____

_____

6. Write down why you believe you made this unconscious commitment. Can you recall an event in your life that may have caused you to make this promise to yourself? As an example, recall my client who was committed to never being alone because her father had threatened to lock her in the basement by herself when she was five years old. If you can't think of the reason in your case, however, don't worry. It may come to you later or with the help of a coach.

_____

_____

_____

_____

_____

_____

7. Write down the many ways this unconscious commitment has interfered with your desires as an adult. What has it cost you? For example, my client Steve was brought up in a Christian household, where making money was seen as valuing the wrong thing. He had a successful and lucrative career but was committed to not making money important to maintain respect for the beliefs he was taught as a child. This commitment has held him back from taking care of his money and benefitting from his investments. He had always wanted to build his dream house, but he couldn't because of this unconscious commitment. At a time in his life when he should have been working less, he was financially in trouble and forced to work even more.

_____

_____

_____

_____

_____

_____

8. Write down how this unconscious commitment kept you safe as a child. What gifts did it bring, even if those gifts no longer serve you as an adult?

_____

_____

_____

_____

_____

_____

9. Take a moment to thank your inner child for keeping you safe by creating your unconscious commitments. Make peace with the fact that this commitment has served you in an important way, even if it's no longer needed. As you've done in previous exercises, gently tell your inner child that it's safe to take the risk and create new commitments that will allow you to have the life you want now. Comfort the child's fears as best you can and remember, you may need to offer this comfort repeatedly.

10. Finally, rewrite your commitment as one that will better serve you as an adult. Here are two examples of unconscious commitments and new commitments that you can use as guides:

> *Unconscious commitment: I have been committed to playing small so that I don't feel judged.*

> *New, conscious commitment: I am now committed to playing big, putting myself out there, and no longer worrying about the judgments of others.*

Unconscious commitment: I have been committed to never becoming trapped in a relationship like my mother.

New, conscious commitment: I am now committed to attracting a great relationship that will allow me to be both loved and free.

Now, write yours:

Unconscious commitment: _____

_____

_____

_____

New conscious commitment: _____

_____

_____

_____

11. I suggest printing out your new commitment and putting it somewhere that you can see it each day. Read it at least every morning and evening to solidify it in your psyche. Continue to read it until you feel you are taking steps toward your leap and beginning to live your bigger life.

12. Finally, revisit the etching exercises from previous chapters, and use them to help you solidify your new empowering commitment.

PERFECTIONISM AND UNCONSCIOUS COMMITMENTS

My client Chloe had a pushy and judgmental mother who forced her to excel in both dance and piano. She could never perform well enough for her mom, though, so Chloe grew up believing she had to be perfect to be acceptable, let alone loved. It caused her to become afraid of trying new things. She didn't feel safe risking imperfection. Her new commitment in adulthood was to try something new and give herself permission to just enjoy it, even if she wasn't good at it.

Then, there's Leah. Her parents were obsessed with her looks. She always had to wear the perfect little dress with matching shoes and bag, and her hair had to be "just so." As a result, Leah grew up with an eating disorder and obsessive-compulsive tendencies. Her unconscious commitment was to always be perfect, which was, of course, impossible.

Many of our unconscious commitments have to do with the fear of being judged, so they activate the tendency toward perfectionism. To a child's mind, it seems we'd be safe if we could only manage to be perfect. No one could judge us then, and we wouldn't be subject to ridicule or abandonment. As we grow up with this thinking, however, it becomes more and more of a slave-driver.

There's certainly nothing wrong with reaching for improvement, of course, but perfection is an ideal that doesn't exist. So irrational striving for some elusive flawlessness can become very self-destructive. As Brené Brown says, "Perfectionism is not the same thing as striving to be your best. Perfectionism is the belief that if we live perfect, look perfect, and act perfect, we can minimize or avoid the pain of blame, judgment, and shame. It's a shield. It's a twenty-ton shield that we lug around thinking it will protect us when, in fact, it's the thing that's really preventing us from flight."[2]

Psychologists seem to agree there are three different types of perfectionists. Those who are *self-oriented* judge themselves based on their own overly high standards. Those who are *other-oriented* become hypercritical and hold the people in their lives to overly high standards. *Socially prescribed* perfectionists try to live up to the high standards they believe others have set.

While each type of perfectionism causes us a great deal of personal pain and keep us from taking our leap in life, they can also bring us gifts. If you're a perfectionist at work, your boss may value you because you perform to a very high standard. What your boss may not know, however, is that you work yourself to the bone and experience anxiety trying always to measure up.

How do you know if you have an unconscious commitment that's related to perfectionism? Here are some examples of perfectionist behavior in daily life:

- Believing you never measure up in life or work.

- Exhaustion as a result of overwork.

- Putting yourself down with frequent critical self-talk.

- Finding it difficult to accept criticism.

- Missing two points on an exam and believing you failed.

- Focusing only on the success (or lack of success) of a project rather than what you learned on the journey.

- Holding yourself to the standard of others' accomplishments.

- Believing anything less than perfect isn't worth doing.

- Frequently criticizing others.

If you feel you have a perfectionist nature, there are ways you can calm down this tendency and give yourself a break. The next time you catch yourself falling into the habit of perfectionism, ask yourself these questions:

1. Is it that important I do this perfectly?

2. If I feel it does matter now, will it matter down the road when all is said and done?

3. What would be the worst-case scenario if I didn't do this perfectly?

4. If the worst happened, where would it truly leave me?

5. Would others see the situation differently?

6. What is a more realistic way to see this?

Here's another way to look more realistically at perfectionism: Stop and think of someone you love. Do they have so-called "flaws" that you find endearing? Maybe you find it amusing that your mom can never remember how to use her phone or your spouse can't ever seem to put a dish in the dishwasher. Don't you think others might look upon some of your imperfections and feel the same—that they give you character and make you who you are? Plus, let's be honest— if someone were truly perfect, wouldn't they be insufferable?

To soften your desire for perfection, try making mistakes on purpose. I know the thought might cause you to shake in your shoes, but that's exactly the idea. Making mistakes will force you to deal with the fearful feelings as they come up, and you'll be able to prove to yourself that you can survive both the fear and the outcome. For example, try:

- Not making your bed for a week.

- Being a few minutes late when you meet with a friend.

- Letting people see your weaknesses and vulnerabilities.

- Not rushing to fill the uncomfortable silences during conversations.

- Putting a post on social media with a typo or two.

- Speaking extemporaneously in a situation where you'd usually rehearse what you planned to say.

- Beginning work on something you've been putting off, and allowing yourself to do it downright badly.

If none of these resonate with your brand of perfectionism, devise your own exercise that will challenge you to stretch beyond the limits that your quest for perfection has put upon you.

Meanwhile, here are some affirmations you can use to calm down perfectionism:

- Nobody is perfect.

- All I can do is my best, and my best is good enough.

- Making a mistake doesn't mean I'm deficient.

- Everyone makes mistakes.

- I love my awesomeness and my "flawsomeness."

- I love myself with all my human imperfections.

- Making a sincere effort is the accomplishment, regardless of ultimate outcome.

Remember to give yourself love whenever you fall into perfectionist tendencies or succumb to an unconscious commitment to stay small. It's just your inner child trying hard once again to keep you safe from harm.

It may take some time to disengage from these promises you made to yourself, but doing this work is the only way I know to make the most out of this life you've been given. I have watched clients prevail over unconscious commitments that were made under the most painful of circumstances and after decades of living within the confines of those commitments. If they can do it, so can you.

LINDA'S STORY

My client Linda was working on lessening her perfectionist tendencies. The action step she chose was to refrain from making her bed four times during the week. The first day she left the house with her bed unmade, she came home after work to meet with a prospective new housekeeper. As Linda walked the housekeeper through the home, emphatically explaining how neat and perfect everything needed to be, she reached the bedroom and was mortified. She tried to explain that the unmade bed didn't reflect her usual way of being. "It was part of an assignment from my coach," she said unequivocally. That's how strong Linda's perfectionism was in her life. To this day, I smile when I picture that scene.

 ## Exercise: Temporal Tapping

Temporal tapping is a particularly powerful way to break old habits. Tapping in this area calms your nervous system and helps your brain become open to your new, empowering commitment.

The premise is that the left hemisphere of the brain responds to affirmations that have a negative word in them. The left side is the "no" side of the brain, so it's more negative and judgmental.

Conversely, the right side is the more positive side, which responds to more positive affirmations. When you speak to each side separately, the effects are stronger than when you use affirmations alone. This helps your unconscious mind get support from your conscious mind.

1. Make a claw with your five fingers, place the claw over your left ear, and tap around your ear with the tips of your fingers from the temple to the back of the ear. Do this five times.

2. Say these affirmations out loud or silently while you tap:

    I no longer need to believe I am not good enough.

    She (he) no longer needs to believe she is not good enough.

    You no longer need to believe you are not good enough.

    We no longer need to believe we aren't good enough.

    [Your name] no longer needs to believe she (he) isn't good enough.

3. Take a deep breath, and repeat two more times before starting on the right side.

4. Now repeat the same tapping sequence five times on your right ear using your right fingers, as you say the following affirmations:

    I choose to believe I am absolutely good enough.

    She chooses to believe she is absolutely good enough.

    You choose to believe you are absolutely good enough.

    We choose to believe we are absolutely good enough.

    [Your name] chooses to believe she (he) is absolutely good enough.

5. Take a deep breath, and notice how you feel.

POINTS TO REMEMBER

Unconscious commitments are promises we make to ourselves to spare ourselves pain and abandonment.

We always get exactly what we're most committed to, regardless of what we *think* or *say* we want. If our unconscious commitment is stronger than our desire as an adult, it's exactly what we'll get.

Unconscious commitments are made for the instant gratification of soothing a wound in the moment. When we look at the commitment consciously and logically, we see that the long-term gratification that's possible *without* the commitment is better for us.

Many of our unconscious commitments have to do with the fear of being judged, so they activate the tendency toward perfectionism.

BIGGER, BETTER, BRAVER MANTRA ACTION

Share the Bigger, Better, Braver mantra with others who might enjoy and benefit from it.

It can be an "inside" mantra with one or more of your friends so that you remind each other to keep thinking it and making choices that will move you toward your vision.

9

STAYING THE COURSE

We start by setting the course, we succeed by staying the course.

—Carece Slaughter

"I would say I was born an artist," Madison says. "I colored on the walls. I colored on the tables. My parents had an expensive set of encyclopedias, and I colored in those. My nursery schoolteacher wrote on my report card, 'Madison is an artist.' But my parents believed you couldn't make money from art, so they said, 'You have to pick something else to study in school.'"

When she went to college, Madison took all her electives in the art department, but after graduation, she took a "regular" job in which she remained unhappy. Years went by, and she got married. But her dissatisfaction with her chosen profession continued. Eventually, she had a conversation with her husband about giving art a try as a money-making profession. "I know I'm supposed to be an artist. I know I could make money at this. If not me, who?" Madison told him. After all, she was *born* to be an artist.

Her husband had a steady income, and they received some money each month from rental properties. So Madison was in the lucky position to make a go of art as a vocation.

"I took art classes again. I started my website," she says. But when she began applying to galleries for an art show, she was inundated with rejections.

"It was horrible," she admits. But she was determined not to quit. Madison reminded herself that Dr. Seuss and *Harry Potter* series author J.K. Rowling both got rejected by many publishing houses before their books were finally accepted and released. "I'm going to make this a defining moment," she told herself. "I'm going to move forward. I know it's a hokey slogan, but 'When one door closes, another one opens.' It's absolutely true. And I've learned it's best not to tightly define what success means to you. If you get rejected by someone, move on to the next one."

Today, Madison's work is displayed in a beautiful gallery in California.

Then, there's Sophia, who had a regular portfolio management job at a firm that was struggling with numerous operating issues. "There were aspects of the job that, even though they were legal, I didn't believe they were ethical or moral," she says. "I wanted to do something more entrepreneurial, new, and creative. I felt if I could control my business, it would be more aligned with my values."

Sophia had plenty of financial fears and was worried that people might not take her seriously since her company would be small. "How would I keep it going every day without the structure I was accustomed to?" she thought. Despite these reservations, she focused on the excitement—the "honeymoon period" of trying something new—and worked on making those feelings stronger than her fears. She reminded herself that the beginning of any project involves uncertainty and awkwardness, and she pushed forward.

Sophia's business worked for seven years, after which she decided to close it down. While that was a disappointment, she's quick to point out that she's much more likely to take another leap toward a new vision now. "From doing something out on my own, I gained so much more confidence and so many different skills. I didn't have the confidence to share and market my own ideas before, and now I do," she says. Today, she enjoys a new job in investor relations on a management team for a biotech firm, and she uses the skills she developed in her own business every day.

Like Madison, Sophia learned that success can look different from what we anticipate when we start on our journey toward our vision. We can't know for sure what will be the magic formula to bring our vision to fruition. Many people have false starts, throwing ten things against the wall before the right one sticks. I, for example, never thought my business would go in the direction it has gone.

As Brian Tracy has said, "You can only grow if you are willing to feel awkward and uncomfortable when you are trying something new." Remember that you might not fit the shoes of your vision at first. You might have to "grow into" those shoes as you learn new skills and expand who you are.

Benjamin (from Chapter 4) has certainly had to regroup and rethink his vision. Do you remember his story? He's the one who started the farm project with a companion luxury resort. Well, the process hasn't been altogether smooth for him or for his team. In fact, some of their original plans haven't worked at all.

Benjamin could have quit. He could have given up. He certainly went through a lot of emotions because of it. "I was really depressed," he says. "I went through shock, frustration, anger, and all the negative emotions mixed up in one. It was like a rug was pulled out from under me. I'd been working toward a singular goal for eight years, and it was always 100% clear no matter how difficult it was that it was definitely happening. Then, all of a sudden, it seemed like it wasn't going to happen. First, I had to accept that the project might not happen, and that made a lot of my pain go away immediately. So just accepting what was happening as opposed to trying to fight 'what is' made me feel a lot better. Then, I was able to start thinking about the path forward, and I had to separate myself from the project. In the beginning, as I accepted that the project might be dying, I felt like a part of *me* was dying. I had to realize that *I* was not the project, and if the project died, my wife and daughter and I would still be alive and would figure out what to do next."

The truth is that your road to your vision may be a winding one. So this chapter is all about staying the course, even when you're uncertain if you will reach your vision.

Exercise: Do You Tend to Quit or Persevere?

This exercise will help you recall your history in terms of perseverance. It isn't an excuse to judge yourself, however. It's a way to discover if you would benefit from developing more resiliencies so that you don't give up too quickly.

1. Recall something you tried to do in the past that didn't come to fruition. What obstacle occurred that caused you to stop? Was it early in the process or after you had given it a lot of time?

   _____

   _____

   _____

_____

_____

_____

2. Think carefully about what happened. Do you think you could have worked harder to move through the obstacle, or do you feel you gave it every possible chance of success?

_____

_____

_____

_____

_____

_____

3. If you believe you could have continued and tried further, what do you think prevented you from giving it more time and effort? Did the obstacle make you feel defeated and afraid you couldn't succeed? Did you face great difficulty that you felt wasn't worth the effort?

_____

_____

_____

_____

_____

_____

4. Recall something else you tried to do that didn't come to fruition. Ask yourself the same questions.

_____

_____

_____

_____

_____

_____

5. Compare the two. Did you behave the same in both circumstances, or did you behave differently? If the same, this is probably a pattern of behavior for you. If different, can you determine why you didn't behave the same? Were you more passionate about one project than the other? Was one of them more difficult than the other?

_____

_____

_____

_____

_____

_____

6. Be honest with yourself, and give yourself love for making the effort to the extent you did. Then, make a commitment to yourself to persevere the next time as much as possible, giving yourself the best possibility of seeing your vision through.

THE WISDOM OF LOW ATTACHMENT

Benjamin's acceptance that his project might not come to fruition is a form of the surrender we discussed in Chapter 3. This acceptance and surrender are exactly what helped him stay in the game and not give up. "I still feel like the project will definitely succeed," he says, "although a part of me knows that it's possible it might not. Knowing that and accepting it is a better focus."

Benjamin is describing a strong work ethic and singular focus on his vision, while also maintaining *low attachment* to the outcome. This is a Buddhist concept that is also a guiding principle of the Law of Attraction. If we're too attached to the outcome, we get in the way of what we want because we're afraid it won't happen. This fear creates tension that not only causes energetic static but makes it harder for us to make sound decisions.

So how do you want something enough to stay motivated and passionate without becoming so attached to it that you fall apart if it doesn't go your way?

It isn't easy. Notice I said *low* attachment rather than *no* attachment. In my experience, it's a tall order to have no attachment whatsoever, but we can do our best to reduce our attachment to the outcome and focus on what we gain from the effort. As I said earlier, *the juice is in the journey.*

When you maintain low attachment, you have a hope, a desire, and a preference for what you would like to happen, but you don't *demand* that it happen exactly as you wish. The best way I know to cultivate low attachment is to develop a greater and deeper trust that the Universe has your back—that everything happens for your greater good to teach you something important, even if you can't discern the lesson right away. Remember: You are exactly where you should be, and everything happens for the evolution of your soul.

Sometimes, as we work toward our leap and our bigger life, we have to rethink our original plans and make adjustments as needed. Whenever we try something new, there will be mistakes and missteps along the way. There's a learning curve for most of us. We can't expect perfection right out of the gate, nor are these obstacles an indication that the Universe isn't supporting us. The Universe always supports us to grow, even if the results aren't on our ego's timeline. Sometimes, we must learn new things before we can reach our final destination. It's easy to look at successful people and imagine they achieved their heights easily. But the truth is: *Successful people are the ones who didn't quit.*

There's still a chance, of course, that Benjamin will end up abandoning his project. If he does, it doesn't mean his leap was unsuccessful. It simply means his quest for a bigger life is far from over. The project he started will be a steppingstone toward the next big thing he wants to try. If that comes to pass, he will have to regroup, listen to his inner voice, create a new vision that considers everything he learned from his previous endeavor, and once again practice low attachment to the outcome.

DISCIPLINE, RESPONSIBILITY, AND CHOICE

One of the issues that often comes up as we work on our vision is lack of *discipline*. It's one of the main reasons people give up. When we lack discipline, it often means we go for immediate gratification rather than wait for long-term gratification. For example, when we overeat, we want the instant gratification of the taste and feeling of fullness. What we sacrifice is the greater long-term gratification of a healthier body.

The same holds true when we procrastinate. We put off doing something that would take us out of our comfort zone for the immediate gratification of not feeling afraid anymore. In the process, we sacrifice the longer-term gratification of stepping out of our comfort zone to fulfill our vision and bigger life. If we allow ourselves to procrastinate long enough, we risk losing all momentum and abandoning our dream altogether.

So discipline requires that we take responsibility for keeping sight of our vision, which may mean delayed gratification. This doesn't mean that you should beat yourself up if you let your discipline slip. That's a recipe for self-sabotage. It's actually a sly way that your scared inner child may try to derail you. Don't let that happen!

Just as you wouldn't go off your diet for backsliding at one meal, don't give up on your vision just because you skipped an action step in favor of procrastination one day. Instead, pick yourself up, brush yourself off, and recommit to what you want to accomplish.

When you feel the urge to go for instant gratification rather than staying the course toward your vision, stop … and ask yourself, "What do I truly want more than anything else?" Is it a donut … or is it long-term health? Is it the comfort of not taking a risk … or is it the bigger, better, braver life of my vision?

Remember: You alone are responsible for making your vision happen. That may feel like bad news, but it's actually good news. It means the power is yours.

You get to determine your own parameters. How far are you willing to go, and how much are you willing to sacrifice? Then, you can make choices from within those parameters. It's your decision how far you will go. But make that decision from a place of courage and expansion rather than from the confines of your comfort zone.

Each choice you make along the way to your vision should serve that vision as best you can. Strive for a healthy balance of focus on your vision, tempered with flexibility for the adjustments you'll need to make, as well as enjoyment of the journey. Just remember that few people reach their vision via a straight line. The story in the section after the next exercise is a case in point!

Homework: Nurture Your Inner Child

As I said in the last section, your inner child's methods for derailing you can be sly and sneaky. This part of you has your best interests at heart, but your child within is misguided about those best interests. And the fear is so pervasive that the child will stop at nothing to stop *you*.

So the next time you feel your inner child is trying to get in your way, ask her what she wants. Then, listen for the answer. It may be that she wants you to stop taking risks, but what she *truly* wants is to feel safe. As you've done in previous chapters, all that's required might be a loving and comforting talk with reassurances from you that all will be okay. Or your child may want you to play a little bit or take some time to be in nature.

If you can find a way to nurture your inner child that doesn't involve abandoning your vision, you may be able to reduce the sneaky interferences. Then, this young part of you may feel more comfortable with waiting for long-term gratification rather than needing immediate gratification to calm her fears.

GET SOME FEEDBACK

In *The Success Principles,* Jack Canfield describes a workshop exercise that shows how often we need to adjust our plans and choices when we reach toward a new vision.[2] He stands at one end of the room and asks someone to volunteer to stand on the opposite side of the room. He puts on a blindfold and takes a step toward the volunteer. He then asks the volunteer to tell him whether he's "on course" or "off course" as he walks toward them one step at a time.

When he receives feedback, he adjusts his steps to try to get back on course. Afterwards, he asks the workshop participants to tell him whether he got more "on course" or "off course" replies.

The answer is always "off course," which shows how often we make mistakes and have to self-correct as we're moving toward our vision. Even with more "off course" replies, however, Jack eventually arrived where he needed to be. The key was staying focused on his vision and being willing to make adjustments while refusing to quit. He didn't judge himself for getting off course or expect he could make it to the other side in a straight line. He simply stayed tenaciously committed to his goal.

As you discover that you need to make adjustments toward your own vision, it can be helpful to get feedback from others. I highly recommend choosing mentors carefully, however. Find people who are knowledgeable in the arena of your vision. If you can find more than one person to give you feedback, all the better. That way, if they give you opposing or significantly different feedback, you will know that their opinions are not definitive. If you receive the same feedback from more than one person, though, you should probably take that feedback seriously.

As I mentioned earlier, it's a good idea for entrepreneurs to get a business coach. In Chapter 5, I mentioned SCORE (Service Corps of Retired Executives), an organization that offers business counseling with experienced volunteers. (There are 63 offices across the U.S. at www.sba.gov/sbdc.)

Whatever your vision, getting honest feedback from others can be an invaluable way to make adjustments. If you aren't sure whether someone's advice is valid, check in with your body and intuition. How does their advice feel? Does it feel "right," or do you feel tension when you think about it? Again, if you aren't sure, try finding someone else in the know to ask for their opinion.

As long as the consequences of the advice won't be significant, though, such as a substantial loss of money, why not give it a try? The worst that can happen is you'll have to adjust again and get yourself back on course.

Don't forget, too, that your inner compass can provide feedback when you're making a decision. Check in with your body. When you think of each choice, what do you feel? Do you feel ease or tension? Do you have any unpleasant sensations? Try to distinguish excitement from caution as you work on becoming more adept at deciphering the messages from your body and intuition. You have probably already had an experience of this when going against your intuition to your detriment. As your skills in this area improve, you will find that your own compass is accurate most of the time.

THE IRONY OF FEAR AS MOTIVATOR

At his heaviest, Jason (from Chapter 2) weighed 330 pounds. Without surgery, he managed to get down to 160 pounds. What motivated him to make that big leap and change his life so dramatically? "Extreme fear," he says. "There was an awakening that was initially started by a fear of dying and a fear of being sick, being on a medically induced diet and drug protocol. And of not being able to have a family and live my life and be a whole person. It's obviously a lower vibrational intent, but it's higher than apathy."

Sometimes, fear is indeed what gets us to move forward. We spend a lot of time working on alleviating our fear. Yet, there are times when it can serve us by not only pushing us out of complacency or apathy but helping us stay on course. Time is going by, and if we don't take action to make our leap, our time in this life will be over. That kind of fear can be a strong motivator.

As I mentioned in Chapter 4, passion isn't always enough to help you take your leap. You must find what motivates *you*. You must find your "*WHY.*"

Your why has to be personal and strong enough to get you to show up over and over again, even when striving for your vision becomes hard. Even when self-doubt and other people's opinions drag you down.

Your why might simply be wanting to live as fully as possible or experience as much joy as you can muster. Or it may be fear of the alternative, as in Jason's case.

What do *you* as an individual need to move you from inaction to action and keep you moving forward despite obstacles on the way? The law of inertia says that an object is likely to remain at rest or in motion unless something happens to change that. So we need something to move us out of the state of inertia because once we're in motion, it's much easier to stay there.

We talked about perfectionism in the last chapter, too, which is one of the primary causes of inertia. We're so afraid we will fail or not live up to expectations that we choose to do nothing. If you stop to think of your life two years from now without any forward movement, fear just may be the positive motivator (the "why) you need—the fear of staying right where you are now.

In other words, over time, the fear that holds you back can give way to the greater fear of not moving forward. There's a heaviness that comes from ignoring what you truly want to do. It becomes like landscape erosion that whittles away at your self-esteem until you have little left. You feel depressed and lethargic, which makes it harder for you to take action. That is why it's so important not to wait until you've been weighted down by disappointment in yourself. If you wait that long, the universe will almost certainly force you to change. Like the breakup of my marriage, something astronomical will happen to push you with full force out of your complacency. Trust me—it's a lot more difficult and painful to make your leap when you have no choice at all.

While I'm not trying to scare you into living bigger, I'm telling you the truth of what can happen. If it takes the fear of going through that to motivate you enough to take action and keep taking action, so be it. That's preferable to the pain of forced change.

You've probably had at least one experience of being forced to change. Maybe you stayed too long in a relationship until it got ugly. Or you refused to leave a job when you knew you should, and it got so bad you couldn't bear it anymore or you were fired. It's never pretty when we resist the change we know we need to make. Ultimately, the result will be unpleasant at best and excruciating at worst.

If you're feeling called to make a change in your life, you owe it to yourself to set a vision and move toward it, even if you shake in your shoes the whole way. It's far better than the alternative and will give you personal satisfaction beyond what any fearful part of you can possibly comprehend.

SETBACKS CAN ACTUALLY BE A BLESSING

For Jason, losing the weight was a huge accomplishment, but it caused another problem he had to solve. He spent so much time in the gym before going to his highly stressful job that he burned out his adrenal glands and became thinner but still unhealthy. He took his weight loss to the other extreme.

"One of the great things about going through an experience like that," he says, "is that you start to build some things like faith, resiliency, and trust. Visiting with each extreme of obesity and adrenal fatigue gave me a lot of awareness of how to balance and optimize my body. It enabled me to really thrive and use my body as a vehicle for spiritual growth, as well as learn how to raise my kids in a natural and healthy way. It also gave me a lot of empathy for people who are overweight because I know how it feels. When you reflect on your life, you see that the things that seem like really deep lows at the time tend to turn into highs. Getting divorced, for example, was an extreme low for me, but it led to my finding a partner who is more suitable for me. Even more importantly, I learned to live by myself and trust in myself. So sometimes, things seem bad, but they're really making way for something new and better."

If you feel your leap isn't going your way, practice trust and patience as best you can. You may find out that the Universe is setting you up for something wonderful beyond your imagination.

 ## Exercise: Reintegrate the Work You've Done Throughout the Book

Revisit what you wrote for the book's first exercise about who you used to be, and revisit what you wrote about your vision. Then, answer the following questions:

1. What do you think is the main shadow belief that has stood in your way of taking a leap toward your vision and bigger life?

    _____

    _____

    _____

    _____

    _____

    _____

2. What do you think is the main unconscious commitment that has stood in your way of taking a leap toward your vision/bigger life?

_____

_____

_____

_____

_____

_____

3. What excuse have you used the most to avoid moving toward your vision and bigger life?

_____

_____

_____

_____

_____

_____

4. How has autopilot gotten in the way of you going for your vision and bigger life?

_____

_____

_____

_____

_____

_____

5. What is your number one fear about going for your vision and bigger life?

_____

_____

_____

_____

_____

_____

6. Now to the more positive part of the exercise: What does faith have to say to you about your vision and bigger life? What words of encouragement does your faith have for you?

_____

_____

_____

_____

_____

_____

7. Write a new belief to counteract the one you wrote for 1.

_____

_____

_____

_____

_____

8. Write a new unconscious commitment to counteract the one you wrote for 2.

_____

_____

_____

_____

_____

_____

9. Spend some time writing here or in your journal about how you feel as you integrate all you've learned and review some of the inner obstacles you face. Do you feel ready? If not, that's okay. You might need to go back through some of the chapters or find a coach to help you through the issues in your way.

_____

_____

_____

_____

_____

_____

10. Remember that with any changes you work toward—resistance, excuses, surrender, fear, beliefs, or commitments—you will no doubt slip from time to time. You are altering long-term habits that are not easy to break. But I'm living proof, along with my clients and friends, that it can be done!

So when you find yourself slipping into your old ways of being, power up with your *Bigger, Better, Braver* mantra, and keep going. Pick yourself up, brush yourself off, and renew your commitment to the life of your choice.

POINTS TO REMEMBER

When you maintain low attachment, you have a hope, a desire, and a preference for what you would like to happen, but you don't *demand* that it happen exactly as you wish.

Successful people are the ones who didn't quit.

Discipline requires that we take responsibility for keeping sight of our vision, which may mean delayed gratification.

Getting honest feedback from others can be an invaluable way to make necessary adjustments.

The fear that holds you back can give way to the greater fear of not moving forward.

BIGGER, BETTER, BRAVER MANTRA ACTION

Turn on music as loud as you can, and dance your heart out to a favorite song like no one is watching. Or do any kind of exercise you like as you say your mantra:

BIGGER, BETTER, BRAVER. I did this recently during hot power yoga, and it felt wonderful.

I promise it will lift your mood, and the mantra will make you feel unstoppable!

10

JUST STEP IN AND TAKE YOUR LEAP

There is no greater gift you can give or receive than to honor your calling.

It's why you were born and how you become most truly alive.

—Oprah

In her book, *Gorge: My Journey Up Kilimanjaro at 300 Pounds*, author and motivational speaker Kara Richardson Whitely wrote about her struggles with binging, food, and weight.[2] Despite these challenges, she has climbed Mount Kilimanjaro not once, but *three* times! And on one of those climbs, she weighed 300 pounds.

"When I was about to turn 30," Kara says, "I got an adventure travel catalog in the mail, and I suddenly realized there was this spark inside of me. Adventure travel is what I love. This is what I want to do."

But Kara had always put off travel or even buying new clothes until she "lost weight" at some hopeful future date.

"Finally, I said to myself, 'I'm about to turn 30, and I'm not getting any younger. So when is that going to happen?'" She decided to start training, beginning with 20-minute hikes on the flat trails in New Jersey.

"I liked how hiking made me feel present again," she says, "because food distanced me from the present. I could feel the breeze on my face and the crunch of the twigs beneath my boots. I could hear the rustle of a stream and be sheltered by the canopy of the forest. Just surrounded by absolute beauty and wonder. Every step might be challenging, but there was such a payoff. Just to be able to take those steps toward health was so powerful."

Kara continued building strength until she was able to hike all the way down the Grand Canyon and back up, as well as Vermont's highest peak and the White Knuckle hike straight down Havasu Falls while holding onto chains and getting soaking wet.

"I allow myself to push for those goals now," she says. "When I was stuck in shadow beliefs, I wouldn't allow myself to feel that beauty, that exhilaration, that pain, or that pleasure. I still have to fight the same initial fears. The inner child reacts, which is automatic, but then, you get to make a choice after that."

Ultimately, Kara's story is about moving mountains. Her vision is now to help others overcome similar obstacles, and her message is ... *if she can do it, so can you.*

Then, there's Brooke. She got married at 28 and stayed in a bad marriage for fifteen years. When she finally got the courage to get a divorce, she remained single for another fifteen years, experiencing several relationships and heartbreaks along the way.

"I decided to take time to look at myself and did a dating hiatus," she says. Brooke worked hard on her fears, beliefs, underlying commitments, and self-love. Two of her shadow beliefs were that life would always disappoint her, and she could never have what she wanted. So one of the ways she protected herself in relationships was to never let her partner know she wanted anything.

Her underlying commitment became to always go for what she knew she could get rather than her heart's true desire. In that way, she felt she could avoid disappointment, but she was disappointing herself constantly by automatically settling for less. She even spent time in a relationship with an addict, as she had a history of doing what she calls "bottom fishing" when choosing men.

To break her patterns, Brooke started asking herself tough questions like "Can I keep my own identity and my own sense of self in a relationship?" "Can I stay true to myself and also be relational?" She was determined to learn how to stay true to herself when coupled with another.

"I knew I wanted to do relationship well. I was very committed to my vision for my life, which included commitment and relationship. And I took responsibility for having conversations from a place of self-worth instead of fear, which would have meant avoiding the truthful conversations altogether," she says.

When she reentered the dating pool, Brooke was able to stay present and practice low attachment on each date. "I had gotten to know my whole self, so I brought my whole self to the table," she says. "I didn't try to be politically correct or worry about frightening my dates off. I was straightforward about who I am and what I was looking for. I told them I come with three kids." Her attitude was that if her true self didn't work for the other person, he wasn't the right one.

Brooke also believes that when you ask the Universe for something, it either says "yes," "you're not ready yet," or "we have something better for you." She says that even if she never achieved the kind of relationship she envisioned, she "would still be in awe of her authenticity."

I'm thrilled to report that Brooke is now happily married. The work she did toward her vision was mostly inner work, compared to the outer work of building a business or preparing to climb a mountain. But her willingness to dig deep within to discover her shadow beliefs, unconscious commitments, and fears is exactly what allowed her to find the right partner and create the relationship she had always longed for.

As you can see, whatever your vision, the steps outlined in this book *work*. They prepare you for the all-important leap toward your vision of a bigger, better, and braver life. But as I said in a previous chapter, *you still have to make that leap*. This is where people often get stuck.

The emotional pain of holding your dream, preparing for it, and then standing still is enormous. When you don't move forward toward your dream and take that final leap, the time that passes steadily diminishes your self-esteem.

In fact, I had a client who couldn't pull the trigger on her leap because her fears were so strong. Eventually, her boyfriend broke up with her because she was unhappy and full of complaints but unwilling to change. The consequences of staying stuck are many.

So in our final pages together, let's do what we can to help you take that all-important final step ... and leap.

SEIZING THE MOMENT

Planning and preparing for your leap can feel like a honeymoon period for many of us. Getting ready for Kilimanjaro was fun. I had my shopping list, reading, and training to do.

While it certainly wouldn't all have been for nothing, it would have been an enormous shame if I hadn't gotten on that plane and at least *tried* to climb the mountain. I would have missed out on that physically challenging but spiritual experience that gave me an entirely new sense of myself and what I'm capable of. To experience that kind of fulfillment, I needed the courage to seize the moment and take my leap.

Kara had to take the leap of getting herself outside and hiking in nature, even though she had to start slowly to build up her strength.

To have the loving relationship she'd always wanted, Brooke had to take the leap of dating from a healthier place.

Remember Madison from the last chapter? She had to take the leap of sending her work to galleries and continuing to do so despite a wave of rejections.

My niece Marni had to take the leap toward weight loss. Now 90 pounds lighter, she runs races she never could before.

My sister had to take the leap of moving to India, where she lived for two years, made incredible new friends, and learned so much from having the courage to live on her own in a foreign country.

So many of my clients and the people I know would have missed out on personal enrichment beyond their wildest imagination if they had not taken that final leap toward their vision for a bigger, better, braver life.

When we don't try, we rob ourselves of what this life is here to offer us. It's ours for the taking if only we accept the gift and step out of our comfort zone.

All the plans in the world will never be enough if you don't complete what you started. Remember: Success comes from taking the leap, and success isn't about the result of the leap. *Taking a leap, in and of itself, spells success.* Even if the outcome doesn't turn out the way you want, success comes from finally taking that leap toward your vision for a bigger life.

For example, I have been working on my business in a way I never planned to do. Even if I decide to follow a new vision in the future, I will consider myself successful. I feel incredible about the work I've done and what I've learned through the process. It feels wonderful to be so busy, learning, trying new things, and bringing my vision to so many people.

Here are just a few of the gifts you'll receive from taking your leap:

- Courage

- Knowledge

- New acquaintances and friends

- Valuable life lessons you'll use the rest of your life

- Personal strength

- Resilience

- Humility

- New confidence

- Self-trust

- Self-love

You'll receive all of these and more regardless of what happens— even if your first leap ends up being a steppingstone toward something bigger still.

In fact, I don't think you can be depressed or unhappy when you've taken your leap toward your vision. You can be scared, tired, or uncomfortable, but not unhappy! And when you're scared, tired, or uncomfortable but moving toward a bigger life, it's a different kind of scared, tired, and uncomfortable than when you're stuck in complacency.

No matter what, your life will be bigger, better, and braver as a result of leaping forward. You will have expanded who you are and what you're capable of.

CHECK YOUR MINDSET

As you move toward the actual moment of your leap, your resistance is likely to be stronger than ever. Your inner child knows it's the moment of truth. It's when you're truly taking a risk, so this is when you'll have to work the hardest on your mindset.

In *Mindset: The New Psychology of Success,* author Carol S. Dweck, Ph.D. says that most of us have either a "fixed" mindset or a "growth" mindset.[3]

People with a fixed mindset tend to only try things when they feel certain they can be successful. For this reason, they're less likely to try something that ventures too far away from what they've done before.

Many people fall into this category without realizing it. They probably did well in school and didn't have to push themselves to get good grades. As a result, they may be highly successful as adults but not risk-takers. If they can't succeed at something naturally without great effort, they aren't likely to challenge themselves.

If you feel you might tend toward a fixed mindset, don't beat yourself up over it! There's nothing inherently wrong with being a fixed mindset person. But I encourage you to begin to make the effort to move toward the *growth* mindset, which will allow you to have the bigger, better, and braver life you're after.

As Dweck puts it, people with a growth mindset have the attitude, "Nothing ventured, nothing gained," while people with a fixed mindset tend to think, "Nothing ventured, nothing lost." I say, much is lost if nothing's ventured.[4]

When we're able to adopt the growth mindset, we let go of perfectionism and see mistakes and false starts as experiences that can lead us to future successes. We're able to see that the juice is in the journey regardless of the ultimate result. When issues arise, we work through them rather than feel defeated.

In fact, some people with a growth mindset are less talented and intelligent than others with a fixed mindset. But the growth mindset provides them with a strong work ethic and quicker recovery when confronted with obstacles. It's a certain brand of resiliency that you can build within yourself.

People with a fixed mindset tend to have a set picture of what success looks like, and nothing else is good enough. With a growth mindset, we see success in our efforts and allow our vision to change and morph into something new along the way. Dweck also says, "In a growth mindset, challenges are exciting rather than threatening. So rather than thinking, oh, I'm going to reveal my weaknesses, you say, wow, here's a chance to grow."[5]

For example, I never thought I'd write a book or become a speaker, but I knew I'd be expected to speak to groups as a coach. So I took a speaking course with Gail Larsen, author of *Transformational Speaking: If You Want to Change the World, Tell a Better Story.*[6] She teaches how to share your story with others. It was an invaluable experience, but it was far beyond the edge of my comfort zone!

Writing a book was equally outside my comfort zone. When I heard about other coaches writing books, I didn't think it was something I wanted to (or could) do. Yet, here I am on the other side of another rewarding experience!

I've come to realize that you may need to get seven steps toward your vision before another door opens in front of you to show you the way. Then, you'll see a new path that you hadn't considered before. Sometimes, you realize that your original vision is just an action step toward a new vision that can't unfold until you've leapt toward the first one. It's "all good," as they say.

While it's important to stay focused on your vision, if you only have your eyes on the "prize" you've specifically identified, you'll miss so much in the moment. And what happens in the moment is an opportunity for you to appreciate and love yourself for having the courage to try something new.

So what can you do if you realize you have a fixed mindset, either all the time or sometimes? Look to people with a growth mindset for inspiration. My sister Ellyn has been that for me. She has long held the inner attitude that she should try anything and could learn whatever she needed to succeed (or fudge it until she owned it). She learned to trust her instincts and her ability to forge ahead no matter the odds. After a failed marriage, she obtained a second graduate degree, launched a second career, and remarried. She became a pilot, boat captain, and active board member of many community organizations. Her way of dealing with conflict and challenges has inspired friends to call on their "inner Ellyn" whenever they were unsure how to proceed. Her growth mindset has served her and others well.

You can also go back to your beliefs and unconscious commitments, and work on them further. If you create new beliefs and commitments that move you away from perfectionism and toward embracing healthy challenges, you will develop the growth mindset you need for your bigger life. This will especially be helpful to you if you find that you're stalling at the moment of taking your leap.

You may need less development than you think to reach for your vision. Much like my sister, Jason eventually understood he was a complete human being with all the qualities he needed inside. He just had to locate them, build on them, and use them. "I already had courage," he says. "I already had resiliency. I already had flourishing." He looked at different times in his life when he had been courageous, disciplined, or resilient and strengthened those characteristics within himself. "It's not like we don't have the courageous gene. It's not like we don't have the hardworking gene. It's getting in touch with the fact that we already have those things," he emphasizes.

If you feel you aren't courageous, remember the times in your life when you had courage. Every time you've applied for a job, gone on a date, or tried something new, for instance, you were courageous. Give yourself credit for what you might dismiss as "small" acts of courage. Revisit your Courage Recall exercise from Chapter 1. You deserve to pat yourself on the back for every moment of courage in your life. They aren't as easy as you'd like to think. The same is true of self-discipline, strength, and resiliency. If you think about your life over the years, you will find experiences where you've exhibited all these qualities. Simply reminding yourself that you've already been brave, strong, and disciplined will help you express those qualities again.

Homework Exercise: Releasing Ceremony

One of my clients did this homework exercise, and I thought it was beautiful. So I wanted to share it with you. You'll need paper, a match or lighter, and a single rose for it.

1. Write all your fears and grievances on a separate piece of paper.

2. Count the number of items you've listed on the paper and gather that many rose petals.

3. Place the paper in a bowl with the petals.

4. Go to a body of water, and as you read each item on your list, drop a rose petal into the water.

5. When you've read all the items and released all the petals, say (out loud if you can): "I release the past, and I am now healed. I thank the Universe for all the lessons and gifts these past experiences have brought me."

6. Burn the paper for the final release.

7. Take a deep breath, and inhale the peacefulness of release. When you exhale, let go of any remaining tension related to any of the items on your list.

SHELLI'S STORY

As the final client story in the book, I want to share Shelli Varela's inspiring experience.

When she left high school, she identified as an artist. "That's how I knew myself. That's how the world knew me," she says.

Then, "by chance," she met with a friend who was a firefighter, and he started to tell her about his job. "I would show up at his house and hang on his every word," she says. "I became obsessed with the job and how it works. I said, 'This is what you get to do every day? Incredible!' I was also interested in the technical part of it. Then, one day, we were driving down the street, and we pulled up next to a tractor-trailer with a dangerous goods placard on the back. I was shy, still a not-so-confident bullied kid on the inside. I didn't want to tell him what the chemical was, even though I was pretty sure I knew it. So instead, I asked him. But he gave me the wrong answer! 'Hmmm,' I said to him, 'I thought it was a class 2 compressed gas and not a class 3 flammable liquid.'"

At that point, Shelli's friend took a clearer look at the placard and realized she had just corrected him. "Why don't you just apply to be a firefighter?" he asked her. "There's going to be a girl one day. Why wouldn't it be you?"

"Do you think I can do it?" she asked him.

Without hesitation, he replied, "Yes!"

This was twenty-eight years ago when there were no female firefighters in her area, so there were no roadmaps for her to follow. "I was a 108-pound manicurist with no skills, knowledge, or experience pertaining to that field," she says. But Shelli wanted it. So how did she do it?

By taking one action step at a time toward her vision. It was 1,162 days of grueling training. She had to learn how to drive a truck and get her body physically capable of doing the demanding work required of a firefighter. She learned fire science, building construction, rescue techniques, and much more.

Shelli says there are plenty of days she felt discouraged. Some days, her body hurt so much that she had to log-roll out of bed. But every time she considered quitting, she connected emotionally to what it would feel like to make the phone call and tell them, "I'm done." She felt she could more easily face the physical pain and emotional uncertainty than she could face the humiliation and disappointment of walking away from something she wanted so much.

Then, on the 1,163rd day, she was offered the job as her city's first female firefighter.

After she had been on the job for a while, someone called in sick, and they asked Shelli to ride with the rescue squad on their most coveted truck. This was a big honor.

When they got called to a house fire, there was a rookie from another truck who was brand new at his first fire. He knew he should be doing *something*, but the atmosphere was so chaotic, he froze. He didn't know what to do.

Shelli's captain said to her, "You see that guy right there? Don't ever be that guy. I would rather you do the wrong thing but with momentum because you can switch on the fly."

The lesson for her that day was "if you have momentum and start down the wrong path, it's easy to switch. Don't wait to take perfect action," she says.

When Shelli was first hired as a firefighter, it was breaking news in her city in Canada. She was on print media, TV, and radio. "Then, one day a lady said to me, 'Thank you so much for sharing your story because I see myself in it. I thought there were things I couldn't do, but now, I'm going to go do them,'" Shelli recalls.

It was then that Shelli realized her story could inspire others to go for what they want against the odds or against logic.

Since then, besides her current job as Fire Captain, she has given a TedX Talk, become a motivational speaker, launched a podcast, and written a children's book. "Not only is it my privilege, but it's my duty to share my story," she says.

If Shelli had maintained a fixed mindset, she might not have been willing to try something so different from the art world she had originally envisioned for herself. With a growth mindset, her life has taken an unexpected turn that has led to countless gifts and blessings for both herself and others.

FINAL WORDS

For each of us, our bigger life is our personal hero's journey. In his book, *The Hero with a Thousand Faces,* Joseph Campbell described the hero's journey like this: "A hero ventures forth from the world of common day into a region of supernatural wonder: fabulous forces are there encountered and a decisive victory is won: the hero comes back from this mysterious adventure with the power to bestow boons on his fellow man."[7]

While you may not have to kill a villain like Voldemort in the *Harry Potter* series or contend with a Cyclops like Odysseus in *The Odyssey,* you will slay your own personal dragons on your quest for a bigger life. You'll reinvent yourself in ways you never dreamed possible. And yes, I do believe you'll have the power to bestow boons on your fellow humans because you'll come out of your journey with new wisdom to share with others. The rewards are beyond expression.

When I was planning my climb up Kilimanjaro, I spoke with a spiritual guide I had first met when in Thailand. I mentioned that I was hoping for a spiritual experience on the climb. His sage advice was simple: "Stay quiet and spend time alone. Allow your feelings to surface without judgment."

It was excellent advice, and I pass it on to you.

As I've said, the call to summit and the journey there and back was the spiritual awakening I wanted. The uncontrollable explosion of joy and gratitude that I felt at the summit, as I gave way to sobs, went through my body in a wave I hadn't expected. Those last steps not only broke me open, but opened me to wholeness.

My colleague Linda Yeazel once remarked that a coaching course we took together left her feeling "broken whole." That's how I felt. My heart opened in a way that it hadn't opened in many years. In the decade prior to climbing the mountain, I noticed it took a lot to make me cry. After reaching the summit, I cried frequently, and the revelations from the experience continued to unfold quietly over a period of months.

I look back on everything now with a sense of awe and wonderment, and I realize that as those tears sprung from my heart, the whole call to summit was my soul's call to self-actualization.

Sharing my experience with my parents was particularly rewarding. They had no concept of what the climb involved, but as I told them more and more about it, I could see the enormity of it unfold in their eyes. I was grateful they were alive to know I did it.

On the plane home from Africa, I looked at the photo of me hugging Abel, my guide, when I received my certificate. It brought me to tears once again, partly out of the deepest gratitude to him for helping me accomplish my dream, but also out of the deepest gratitude to myself for having the gumption to make it to the summit and down again. On that journey home, I wrote: "I am never alone because I always have me. I don't need to be afraid because I always have me. I am so in love with who I am. I know there will always be more work to be done, but for now, I feel complete."

One of the biggest contributors to my feeling of accomplishment was knowing I stayed in integrity with my word. I didn't just prepare and give in to fear. I kept going and took my final leap, and I can't even begin to describe how much better I am (and yes, braver) for having done that.

It's the things we're willing to take on in life that define who we become. Where do you want to watch the world from? The couch? The sidelines? Or the trenches? *The profound lesson is in the doing.*

As you prepare for your leap, for your bigger life, you open yourself up to your wounds and fears. That alone is courageous. Every person who has become a coach has made that leap, and everyone I've coached has done it. Revisiting my clients' journeys with them for this book has been an unexpected gift of the writing process. It has been an emotional experience, and I've felt so proud of each of them. People like my client Carol, who now has forty people working for her and is traveling around the world giving talks and moderating events. People like Brooke, Amanda, Steve, Madison, Chloe, Ruth and Shelli.

The mere act of hiring a coach is a move toward living a bigger life. That alone can be your leap! It's such a life-altering experience, however, that it will probably lead to yet another leap for you.

Whether you climb Kilimanjaro, start a new business, reach for the relationship you've always wanted, or simply try something new that expands who you are beyond your current confines, it's a transformative event.

After my leap, my self-confidence was solid. My self-love was constant and unwavering. It was a life-changing breakthrough. I went to Africa as one person and returned another. Reaching for your bigger, better, braver life will be the same for you.

You will start toward your vision as one person and emerge from the other side of it as someone new and renewed.

"Twenty years from now, you will be more disappointed by the things that you didn't do than the ones you did do.

So throw off the bowlines. Sail away from the safe harbor.

Catch the trade winds in your sails. Explore. Dream. Discover."

—H. Jackson Brown, Jr.[8]

I strongly urge and encourage you to find your own personal call to summit and make it happen—*bigger, better, and braver.*

EPILOGUE

Ten days after I submitted my manuscript to Teri Rider at *Good Reads Publishing*, my sons invited me to participate in a sweat lodge with them and their partners. My son Jason remarked that the sweat lodge experience would be in keeping with my Bigger, Better, Braver attitude. His comment rang true.

We were gathering in upstate New York at his new home, and all three of my grandchildren would be there. I didn't hesitate to accept the invitation.

Usually when we're all together, I opt to babysit the granddaughters. I don't often get to enjoy the east coast and west coast kids in the same place. But I realized that always being with the grandchildren kept me from doing things with my adult children.

I didn't know what to expect from the sweat lodge. I had concerns after reading that people have died in them. But I trusted my kids would source a reputable guide, and I surrendered to the experience, assuming it would bring me something I needed.

The woman leading the sweat lodge treated us to an informative history of the practice and her lineage as a guide. We then went outside and arranged ourselves in a circle outside the sweat lodge in front of a roaring campfire filled with large stones. The men, referred to as grandfathers, sat on one side, with the women, referred to as grandmothers, on the other.

The leader met individually with each of us to ask what questions we had for our ancestors and our intentions for the day. She said for me to be invited and willing to participate in this heart-opening experience with my children meant I must be doing something right. Her comment made me realize how far we had all come. This recent visit with my children had been the smoothest we'd ever had. We had been working on ourselves individually as well as within our relationships, and it showed. I felt deep gratitude for the clarity of doing what's right.

Finally, the fire and stones became hot enough to move us into the sweat lodge, a dome like hut covered with heavy blankets. One by one, they brought the large hot stones into the lodge and placed them in the middle. When all eight stones were transferred, they dropped the blankets, submerging us in total darkness.

Before we began, the leader told us that no one has ever died or gotten sick in her lodge. She pointed out that when we feel on the brink and can't take anymore, we're getting the most "medicine" and healing from our ancestors. In my book, I speak about how people quit when on the precipice of reaching their goal. Remembering that gave me the courage and strength to stay. It was a profound moment.

The leader sprayed the stones with water and herbs, filling the interior air with scented steam. She sang a few beautiful chants as the heat increased. As it became hotter and hotter, my heartbeat raced, so I used breathing techniques to calm myself.

Before long, she signaled to open the door, marking the end of round one. They lifted a few blankets, allowing air to rush in all around us. The cool air sweeping into the lodge was a gift. I expected to leave the tent between rounds, but we stayed.

I had concerns that the heat might increase with each successive round. Regardless, I had to be with it. Round two was hotter, and we each struggled but endured.

Round three brought me to an epiphany. Bigger, Better, Braver is more than choosing a big jump and following through. It's more than a mantra to repeat. It's a way of life, living with the intention to choose Bigger Better Braver each day and each chance we get. It's saying Yes to Us and Yes to Life.

We ended the final round with a ceremony, and the leader challenged us to reflect on the value of our lives. She said that when we die, our creator will ask these questions.

Did you live life to its fullest?

Did you help others less fortunate than yourself?

How did you contribute to the world?

The sweat lodge with my children was no random event. It was the perfect ending to my book, opening me to an awareness I needed. The Universe gave me both the title for my book and brought me the ending, too. Thank you, Universe.

As for the future, I look forward to the "me" that has yet to unfold, and I'm excited for the new "you" that will unfold as you commit to living Bigger Better and Braver.

In light and love,

Nancy

Thank you for reading!

Dear Reader,

I hope you enjoyed **Bigger Better Braver**.

As an author, I appreciate getting feedback. I would enjoy hearing your thoughts and your own stories of your experiences becoming bigger, better, and braver. You can write me at the addresses below.

Like all authors, I rely on online reviews to encourage future sales. You, the reader, have the power to influence other readers to share your journey with a book you've read. In fact, most readers pick their next book because of a review or on the advice of a friend. So, your opinion is invaluable. Would you take a few moments now to share your assessment of my book on Amazon, Goodreads or any other book review website you prefer? Your opinion will help the book marketplace become more transparent and useful to all.

Thank you so much for reading **Bigger Better Braver**. And if you are so inclined, please visit my website to learn more about my work and follow me on social media.

You can visit me online at: https://nancypickardlifecoach.com

Email me at: nancy@nancypickardlifecoach.com

Instagram: @nancypickardlifecoach

Facebook: @nancypickardlifecoach

ABOUT THE AUTHOR

Nancy Pickard is a Certified Integrative Coach through The Ford Institute for Transformational Training. She is certified as a Breakthrough Shadow Coach, Empowered Parent Coach, Courage Coach, Healing Your Heart Coach, Leadership Coach, and Holistic Lifestyle Coach.

Before becoming a life coach, she founded and owned a personal training gym called Tight Ends, operating it by herself for sixteen years. She knows what it takes to help people achieve big goals.

Nancy splits her time between Aspen, Colorado and Larkspur, California. She is the mother of two sons, the grandmother of three girls, and the happy owner of an irrepressible Australian Labradoodle named Bliss.

Nancy was born and raised in Buffalo, New York and is the youngest of three girls. She is an enthusiastic athlete, and when not working, she can be found hiking, road biking, skiing or practicing yoga. At the age of 61, Nancy climbed Kilimanjaro as part of her personal pursuit for a Bigger, Better, Braver life.

SPECIAL RECOGNITION

I never met Debbie Ford, as she was leaving this earth when I first began coaching. As an Integrative Life Coach at the Ford Institute and Head of Mentor training, however, her work heavily influenced my early learnings and her books and coaching manuals are instrumental in my book. I am grateful for her impact. Her brilliance has helped millions, and I'm honored to be among those sharing it.

ACKNOWLEDGMENTS

With deep gratitude, I want to thank everyone who helped get this book off the ground and supported me throughout my journey.

To my parents, Claire and Irving, you are my rock. You have never wavered as my greatest cheerleaders. My moral code, resiliency, determination, and strength come from your collective guidance and shining example. I am as proud of you as you are of me. Your legacy has already sprouted deep roots and will continue to bless and enhance generations to come with love. I would not be who I am without the two of you. Thank you, and love always.

To my sons, Jason and Jared, you are my greatest accomplishments. I am in awe of how you stand in the world. I especially admire the depth and manner of your love for your families. I wanted you to grow up as loving men and accomplish your dreams, and you've never let me down. You each have traveled your hero's journey and inspired me to greater heights in the wake of your accomplishments. Thank you for reading my manuscript and offering your much appreciated and respected suggestions. And thank you for keeping me on my game and pushing me to be more.

To my sisters, Ellyn and Betsy, Mom's greatest wish was that we would be best friends for all time and support each other always, and that wish came true. Our strength and bond have never felt stronger than in the past few years. I have always felt your support and love, and as your (much younger) sister, could never want for more than what I receive from each of you. We are blessed to have each other.

To Velisa and Kara, my daughters (in-law). I always wanted daughters, and I came to learn how great it is to have two remarkable daughters-in-law, who are daughters and friends all wrapped up together. I couldn't be more blessed than having you two in my life. Thank you for loving my sons. I desperately needed teammates and will forever be there to support you and know you are there for me.

To Manola, Kaya, Anjah, and Khijra, there can be no greater gift than you. Being your Nana is my greatest joy. I rejoice in our unconditional love and am blessed to have you.

To Michael Coffino, my deepest thanks for being such a beautiful partner in my life. I can't imagine doing this without your support and guidance. You calm my crazy days and offer love always. I am in awe of your ability as a writer and thank you for your editorial genius. I greatly appreciate and value the time and effort you devoted to editing my manuscript. I love you, Babe.

To my posse of girlfriends who have made this journey with me, I could never have done it without you. I would love to name you all, but I'm blessed with so many dear friends. I have always said I'm a girl's girl. Life would not be nearly as colorful or joyful without you. You have each been a constant source of support. My East Coast girls have been with me through it all, and I appreciate your love and support. My Aspen and California girls have been added treasures to my tribe. Thanks to all of you for being there for me and with me. You are truly the backbone of my life.

To my Ford Institute Family—Kelley Kosow, Julie Stroud, Vincent Scotto, Linda Yeazel, Nancy Levin, Linda Perry, Laura Summers, and Michael Mammina—it has been an honor and pleasure to share this professional journey with you. Your support and teaching are unmatched and immense, and I hope it never ends. I love our Ford Family and am honored to help bring our work to the world.

Thank you to Gail Larson for helping me find my "original story" and recognize I had a story to share and an obligation to do so.

A special thank you to Nancy Levin for telling me my book should be much more than a tale about my ascent up a daunting mountain and more about the work I do as a life coach in the spirit of

"What's Your Kilimanjaro?"

To Melanie Votaw, you held my journey in your hands and were essential in helping me craft this book. You are a skilled artist. I couldn't have done it without you, nor would I have wanted to.

To Wendy Sherman, you have been with me each step of the way. Who knew when we first became friends so many years ago that your calling as a book agent would someday support a dream I never knew I had?

Thank you, Marissa Harris. Thank you for everything. You were my first Ford Coach, introduced me to this "work," and inspired me to become a coach. I will be forever grateful.

A special shout out to my Kilimanjaro porter, the amazing Abel August Tarimo. You made climbing Kilimanjaro epic. Because of you, I felt safe and held throughout the journey, and your beautiful smile buoyed me every day. It was a gift to listen to you quietly singing the Kilimanjaro song "Jambo" whenever you heard me practicing it as we walked. I would not have wanted to reach the summit with anyone but you.

To those who contributed their stories to my book and all my clients, the greatest gift of the interviews during the writing of this book was recognizing and enjoying how each of you is living a Bigger, Better, Braver life. As I listened to your stories and revisited our coaching relationships, I was awed by how brave you are. Listening to the interviews, I fell in love with each of you. The mere act of hiring a coach to work on yourself was an act of bravery and a gift you gave yourself. Thank you for trusting me and allowing me to accompany you on your journey. I appreciate your willingness to share your stories in the spirit of helping others. You are all courageous warriors, and there would be no book without you.

Thank you Teri Rider of Top Reads Publishing for having my back throughout the process of bringing my book to the world. Your professionalism and personal care made the process painless, and I am most grateful.

I also want to thank my readers. Your desire and willingness to grow and become all you are meant to be inspired this book. You, too, are courageous warriors. I hope this book supports you in your quest to live a bigger, better, braver life.

Lastly, thank you to the Universe for helping me grow and evolve to the woman I am today. Every trial has made me stronger, and I've been blessed with so many gifts. I trust in your abundance, and I appreciate your constant support. I know that whatever comes my way, it will be for the evolution of my soul. I am grateful.

NOTES

Introduction

1. Epigraph
   Campbell, Joseph (January 3, 2020) https://www.goodreads.com/ quotes/143093-follow-your-bliss-if-you-do-follow-your-bliss-you

2. Ford, Debbie (2006) *Spiritual Divorce: Divorce as a Catalyst for an Extraordinary Life* HarperOne.

Chapter 1

1. Epigraph
   Boone, Louis (December 28, 2019) https://www.gauraw.com/the-saddest-summary-of-life-contains-3-descriptions-could-have-might-have-and-should-have/

2. Levin, Nancy (2014) *Jump . . . And Your Life Will Appear: An Inch-by-Inch Guide to Making a Major Change.* Hay House, Inc., p. 92.

3. Van Dyke, Henry (December 28, 2019) https://www.bookbrowse.com/ quotes/detail/index.cfm/quote_number/433/use-what-talents-you-possess-the-woods-would-be-very-silent-if-no-birds-sang-there-except-those-that-sang-best

4. Jeffers, Susan (2006) *Feel the Fear and Do it Anyway.* Ballantine Books.

5. Walsch, Neale Donald (December 28, 2019) https://www.beaconsofchange.com/end-of-your-comfort-zone/

Chapter 2

1. Epigraph
   Gurdjieff, G.I. (December 28, 2019) https://www.goodreads.com/ quotes/6802800-you-are-in-prison-if-you-wish-to-get-out

2. Kosow, Kelley (2017) *The Integrity Advantage: Step Into Your Truth, Love Your Life, and Claim Your Magnificence.* Colorado: Sounds True.

3. Crane, Rebecca (2017) *Mindfulness-Based Cognitive Therapy.* New York: Routledge.

4. Phillippa Lally, Cornelia H.M. Van Jaarsveld, Henry W.W. Potts and Jane Wardle, *How are habits formed: Modelling habit formation in the real world,* European Journal of Social Psychology Eur. J. Soc. Psychol. 40, 998–1009 (2010) Published online 16 July 2009 in J. Wiley Online Library

5. Ford, Debbie (2003) *The Right Questions: Ten Essential Questions to Guide You to an Extraordinary Life.* New York: HarperCollins Publishers, p. 65.

6. Quotes based on personal interviews.

Chapter 3

1. Epigraph
   Harvey, Andrew (December 28, 2019) https://thebrickmagazine.com/surrender/

2. Jung, Carl (December 28, 2019) http://www.happinessinsight.com/mindfulinsights/whatyouresistwillpersist

3. Ford, Debbie (2009) *Why Good People Do Bad Things: How to Stop Being Your Own Worst Enemy,* HarperOne; Reprint edition, p. 6.

4. Stutland, Erin (2019) *Mantras in Motion: Manifesting What You Want Through Mindful Movement.* New York: Hay House, Inc.

5. *Courage Coaching Manuel: The Ford Institute for Transformational Training* (2013).

6. *Courage Coaching Manuel: The Ford Institute for Transformational Training* (2013).

7. Canfield, Jack (2015) *The Success Principles: How to Get from Where You Are to Where You Want to Be.* New York: HarperCollins Publishers, p. 191.

8. Singer, Michael (2007) *The Untethered Soul,* New Harbinger Publications/ Noetic Books.

Chapter 4

1. Epigraph
   Rohn, Jim (December 28, 2019) https://www.brainyquote.com/quotes/jim_rohn_121478

2. Kosow, Kelley (2017) *The Integrity Advantage: Step Into Your Truth, Love Your Life, and Claim Your Magnificence.* Colorado: Sounds True, p. 75.

Chapter 5

1. Epigraph
   Franklin, Benjamin (December 28, 2019) https://www.brainyquote.com/quotes/benjamin_franklin_138217

2. Thomas, Katherine Woodward (2016) *Conscious Uncoupling: 5 Steps to Living Happily Even After* Harmony; Reprint edition.

3. Thomas, Katherine Woodward (2016) *Conscious Uncoupling: 5 Steps to Living Happily Even After* Harmony; Reprint edition.

4. Ford, Debbie (2006) *Spiritual Divorce: Divorce as a Catalyst for an Extraordinary Life* HarperOne.

Chapter 6

1. Epigraph
   Mandela, Nelson (1994) *Long Walk to Freedom*, Little Brown @ Co.

2. Proctor, Bob (December 28, 2019) https://www.goodreads.com/quotes/5099913-faith-and-fear-both-demand-you-believe-in-something-you

3. Heller, Robert (December 28, 2019) https://www.brainyquote.com/quotes/robert_heller_160121

4. Maslow, Abraham (December 28, 2019) https://www.goodreads.com/quotes/118145-one-can-choose-to-go-back-toward-safety-or-forward

5. Ford, Debbie (2012) *Courage: Overcoming Fear and Igniting Self-Confidence.* New York: HarperCollins Publishers, p. 55.

6. Heller, Robert (December 28, 2019) https://www.brainyquote.com/quotes/robert_heller_160121

7. Ford, Debbie (2012) *Courage: Overcoming Fear and Igniting Self-Confidence.* New York: HarperCollins Publishers, p. 55.

Chapter 7

1. Epigraph
   Brown, Les (December 28, 2019) https://www.brainyquote.com/quotes/les_brown_379156

2. Whitely, Kara Richardson (2015) *Gorge: My Journey Up Kilimanjaro at 300 Pounds*, Hatchett Book Group.

3. *Breakthrough Shadow Coaching Manuel: The Ford Institute for Transformational Training* (2017).

Chapter 8

1. Epigraph
   Ford, Debbie (December 28, 2019) https://www.brainyquote.com/quotes/debbie_ford_712258

2. Brown, Brené (December 28, 2019) https://www.goodreads.com/quotes/987280-perfectionism-is-not-the-same-thing-has-striving-to-be

Chapter 9

1. Epigraph
   Slaughter, Carece (December 28, 2019) https://i.pinimg.com/originals/78/b8/e9/78b8e92c031bb73045ba651dde4559b5.jpg

2. Canfield, Jack (2015) *The Success Principles: How to Get from Where You Are to Where You Want to Be.* New York: HarperCollins Publishers, p. 191.

Chapter 10

1. Epigraph
   Oprah (December 28, 2019) https://www.azquotes.com/quote/615789

2. Whitely, Kara Richardson (2015) *Gorge: My Journey Up Kilimanjaro at 300 Pounds*, Hatchett Book Group.

3. Dweck, Carol S. (2006) *Mindset: The New Psychology of Success.* New York: Random House Publishing Group, p. 33.

4. Dweck, Carol S. (2006) *Mindset: The New Psychology of Success.* New York: Random House Publishing Group, p. 16.

5. Dweck, Carol S. (December 29, 2019) https://hbr.org/2012/01/the-right-mindset-for-success

6. Larson, Gail (2009) *Transformational Speaking: If You Want to Change the World, Tell a Better Story*, Celestial Arts, Reprint Edition.

7. Campbell, Joseph (January 3, 2020) https://www.goodreads.com/quotes/824449-a-hero-ventures-forth-from-the-world-of-common-day

8. Brown Jr., H. Jackson, (December 28, 2019) https://quoteinvestigator.com/2011/09/29/you-did/

REFERENCES

Campbell, Joseph (2008) *The Hero with a Thousand Faces* New World Library; Third edition.

Canfield, Jack (2015) *The Success Principles: How to Get from Where You Are to Where You Want to Be.* New York: HarperCollins Publishers.

Chek, Paul (2018) *How to Eat, Move and Be Healthy*, C.H.E.K Institute; 2nd edition.

Crane, Rebecca (2017) *Mindfulness-Based Cognitive Therapy.* New York: Routledge.

Dweck, Carol S. (2006) *Mindset: The New Psychology of Success.* New York: Random House Publishing Group.

Ford, Debbie (1998) *The Dark Side of the Light Chasers: Reclaiming your power, creativity, brilliance, and dreams.* New York: Riverhead Trade.

Ford, Debbie (2003) *The Right Questions: Ten Essential Questions to Guide You to an Extraordinary Life.* New York: HarperCollins Publishers.

Ford, Debbie (2006) *Spiritual Divorce: Divorce as a Catalyst for an Extraordinary Life*, HarperOne.

Ford, Debbie (2009) *Why Good People Do Bad Things: How to Stop Being Your Own Worst Enemy*, HarperOne; Reprint edition Ford, Debbie (2012) *Courage: Overcoming Fear and Igniting Self-Confidence.* New York: HarperCollins Publishers.

Ford, Debbie (2012) *Courage: Overcoming Fear and Igniting Self-Confidence.* New York: HarperCollins Publishers.

Jeffers, Susan (2006) *Feel the Fear and Do it Anyway.* Ballantine Books

Kosow, Kelley (2017) *The Integrity Advantage: Step Into Your Truth, Love Your Life, and Claim Your Magnificence.* Colorado: Sounds True.

Larson, Gail (2009) *Transformational Speaking: If You Want to Change the World, Tell a Better Story*, Celestial Arts, Reprint Edition.

Levin, Nancy (2014) *Jump . . . And Your Life Will Appear: An Inch-by-Inch Guide to Making a Major Change.* Hay House, Inc.

Lewis, Mike (2018) *When To Jump: Ditch the Day Job, Pursue Your Passion and Create a Life You Love.* London: Hodder & Stoughton.

Phillippa Lally, Cornelia H.M. Van Jaarsveld, Henry W.W. Potts and Jane Wardle, *How are habits formed: Modelling habit formation in the real world,* European Journal of Social Psychology Eur. J. Soc. Psychol. 40, 998–1009 (2010) Published online 16 July 2009 in J. Wiley Online Library.

Singer, Michael A. (2007) *The Untethered Soul,* New Harbinger Publications/ Noetic Books.

Stutland, Erin (2019) *Mantras in Motion: Manifesting What You Want Through Mindful Movement.* New York: Hay House.

Thomas, Katherine Woodward (2016) *Conscious Uncoupling: 5 Steps to Living Happily Even After* Harmony; Reprint edition.

Walsch, Neale Donald (2005) *The Complete Conversations with God,* TarcherPerigee.

Whitely, Kara Richardson (2015) *Gorge: My Journey Up Kilimanjaro at 300 Pounds,* Hatchett Book Group.